Baby Names:

2'500 Original names to pick the right one for your soon to be born baby

Table of Contents

Introduction 6

Chapter 1: How to Choose the Right Name for Your Baby 8

1 NAMESAKES CAN BE CONFUSING 8
2 LENGTHY NAMES 9
3 DIFFICULT TO SPELL OR PRONOUNCE 9
4 FUNNY NAMES OR NICKNAMES 10
5 UNISEX NAMES 11
6 MEANINGS 11
7 UNIQUENESS 12
8 POPULARITY 12
9 STEREOTYPES 12
#10 GENDER 13

Chapter 2: Choosing Names by Continent 14

1. EUROPE 14
2. AFRICA 59
3. NORTH AMERICA 64
4. SOUTH AMERICA 71
5. ASIA 83

Chapter 3: Trendy Names 105

Chapter 4: Big Screen Character Names   110

Chapter 5: Mix the Gender   124

Chapter 6: Heroine Names   127

Chapter 7: Heroes Names   131

Conclusion   136

The information herein is offered for informational purposes solely, and is universal as so. The presentation of the information is without contract or any type of guarantee assurance.

The trademarks that are used are without any consent, and the publication of the trademark is without permission or backing by the trademark owner. All trademarks and brands within this book are for clarifying purposes only and are the owned by the owners themselves, not affiliated with this document.

Introduction

Giving a name to a baby seems a simple task but it brings a mixture of expressions and emotions to the one giving it. It can also be an overwhelming responsibility when you know that your child will forever be intertwined with that name. So most often, especially when it's the first child in the family, parents would make a fuzz over what name to choose for the coming baby.

The first time the babies were introduced to their names, that's their first baptism and just imagine the joy of the parents while picking names to give their baby. Every name got its own character and breadth. But more than everything, a name you give to your child is an extension of yourself. You choose it based on your preference, your likes, your culture, your belief. The name you give to your baby will influence him greatly just as you are a great influence to your child's life.

If you want your child to stand out from the crowd, give him a unique name and at the time you baptized him with the name you had chosen, you are breathing into his life what you want him to be by way of choosing names which you can relate to.

In this book, "Baby Names: 2'500 Original names to pick the right one for your soon to be born baby" is a collection of names gathered from various resources across different times, ages, gender, places, culture, and ideas along with their relevant meanings in our aim to help you make a perfect name for your baby.

Every section of this eBook imparts a realization that names are not just pieces of words tied together so you can have something to call your baby. A name is a representation of who you are and what you want your child to be.

Chapter 1: How to Choose the Right Name for Your Baby

Whatever you want to give to your baby, you make sure you want to give him the best. This includes giving him the best of the names you can think. Whether you want him to stand out or just blend with the crowd, you surely want to give him a name that is special, significant and worthy of him.

Giving your child his name especially when he is your first-born could be extremely overwhelming. You prepare to give him the name even months before his arrival, even when you are not yet sure of his gender.

Before you start picking up a name for your child, here are some things you may want to consider so you can avoid giving your child a name that could serve him some difficulty in life as he grows older.

1 Namesakes can be Confusing

Giving your baby a name which is an exact replication of someone you want to be truly remembered can be confusing even if you will be adding, "Jr.", "II, III, IV …" Even when your child carries your middle name to distinguish him from his father, still it will create confusion especially when they both happen to have the same initials.

Worst than that is the fact that your child will never get the satisfaction of having his own identity. Others will continue to see him as the shadow of his namesake.

To some parents, it is important to follow some tradition or religion in naming their child. Roman Catholics traditionally chose names of saints and using Mary for first came while adding another name like Mary Rose, Mary Jane, Mary Joy. Maria can also be used instead of Mary for Latin version Maria Isabel, Maria Mirasol, Maria Clara, and Maria Inez. By tradition, Jews are choosing Old Testament names in naming their children while Protestant religion chooses names that both came from the Old and New Testament. Muslims, on the other hand, turn to Koran and the names of Mohammed and his family as part of their tradition.

So make sure that the namesake's name you choose is one that you have chosen on its own merits, apart from the feeling for the one you're complimenting this way.

2 Lengthy Names

Some people can choose long and foreign-sounding names. Unknowingly, the name they had picked for their child can cause him great difficulty.   Imagine if your child's name is Juan Carlo Barcelona y Divinagracia. By the time he starts learning to write his name, he could have a hard time mastering and scribbling all those lengthy letters.

3 Difficult to Spell or Pronounce

If the name is foreign-sounding, be sure that your child or other people won't find it hard to spell or pronounce them. Surely no one wants to have his or her name constantly mispronounced. A name like Jesus could be pronounced in different ways depending on where you live. If you are an American, you are more likely to be called,

'Gee-sus', but for Latin countries, they probably prefer to be called 'He-soos'.

If you choose a name that sounds foreign-sounding, be sure that it's neither unpronounceable nor "unspellable", else you just make it a burden to your child.

Combinations of names in other countries can sounds funny or eerie, especially when you have no idea how they are pronounced correctly.

4 Funny Names or Nicknames

Most people have short names or familiar names given to them either by their parents or friends or anyone familiar to them. They could be a form of endearment or a product of imagination, emotion or some unusual events in a person's life.   Sometimes, these names can change in some stages. You can call Michael, 'Mickey' as a child, 'Mikc' when he reach his teenage life, and 'Mikaelo!' when you in a burst of anger. So when you don't want your daughter to be called "Sam", don't name her 'Samantha.'
Namesakes can also lead to unfortunate choices especially when it doesn't fit your child's personality. A name like Donato doesn't seem to fit a little boy comfortably when it perfectly fits a young Gentleman or rich older men residing in a villa.

There are some nicknames that can provoke smiles to other people's faces. Though this rarely happens, there are parents who love to make a joke out of their children's names. Nicknames are often provided a joke or for fun.

The same holds true for initials. How would you want your child's initial to be like

A.S.S., I.L.L., L.O.L.! Most often, it's too late when you realized that the joke is on your baby's name and he will be bearing it like a curse for the rest of his life.

5 Unisex Names

Some parents just want to play safe when they think ahead of what names they will give their baby. So, they choose a name that can either be changeable like Carol or Caroll, Lesley or Leslie, Claire or Clair. Some even go to the extent of giving unisex names like Jessie, Robin, Chris, and Terry.

6 Meanings

Every name has its meaning. Most people don't know what their name means or they simply don't mind. However, if you don't want to give your children embarrassing names, at least, research for their meanings before.

Some religious sects believe that the meaning of every name is important as it has some spiritual implications. An example is Mara which means bitter. They believe that by giving your child this name, she will be living a bitter life. Whether there's some truth in that or not, you don't want your daughter's life to be bitter. Avoid giving names that connotes negativity or adversity.

#7 Uniqueness

It is important that your child's name is unique even if he or she can go with the crowd. Nevertheless, it's better if the name that you give to your kid can make him or her stands out in the crowd. Just imagine how ridiculous it can be if your name child John Doe or Jane Doe which are typical American placeholders' names for unknown personalities.

A unique name can give your child a unique personality. Even names created for namesakes can steal the sense of identity from your child as he will always feel like living in the shadow of someone's else.

#8 Popularity

You may want to choose a name that is popular or gives your child a name taken after popular people. Just remember that names like these are not unique because of their popularity. When your child goes to school, he will soon find out there's a dozen of John or Joe's out there that he would prefer to stay silently in the background.

Names taken after popular people may soon lose its popularity and what's worst is when some popular people make their exit on public's opinion, they leave scandalous memories. This can somehow tarnish the name you had chosen.

#9 Stereotypes

Most names call to mind personalities of personality traits that stem from a well-known namesake, real or in fiction.

Take, for instance, Adolf or Judas, who were terribly associated with some events you may not want to associate yourself with.

It's good if you name your child Helen after Helen of Troy, who seems not to outlive the face that had launched a thousand ship, or Einstein whom you can easily equate with floating numbers or inventions.

Older people would say, you can bear the traits of your namesakes. Hence, if you want your kid to be like Einstein, then name him. If you want him to be a great leader, name him Napoleon or after some prominent leaders, we have in our history.

#10 Gender

When it comes to names that can be given to boys and girls alike, there can be two contradicting thoughts whether they can be interchanged like Leslie/Leslie. Bobby/Bobbie, Claire/Clair or they can be easily identifiable like Teresa, Jose, Robin.

Nonetheless, there are names that are still confusing like Joey as it can be used by both sexes. This kind of name is commonly chosen in other countries like Africa who have names that can be used by both sexes.

Some parents choose in advance names they want to give to their baby. Without the use of ultrasound, you can never be sure if you baby will be a boy or a girl. Hence, to play it safe, parents chooses names that can either be applicable to both or sounds the same but they can make a simple twist later with the spelling.

Chapter 2: Choosing Names by Continent

Choosing a name for your baby can be governed or influenced by culture, hence, people from every continent in general, and country, in particular, chooses a name in their own language. But because of the interracial marriages and western influences in culture, names given to babies are now too diversified.

◼ Girl Names	◻ Boy Names	▢ Unisex Names

1. EUROPE

BABY NAMES	COUNTRY	MEANING
Yllka	Albania	Little star
Ylli	Albania	Star
Letje	Belgium	Tiny and womanly
Salina	Belgium	Silent
Desislav	Bulgaria	Glory
Kamen	Bulgaria	Stone
Lala	Bulgaria	Tulip

BABY NAMES	COUNTRY	MEANING
Violeta	Bulgaria	Violet
Remei	Catalonia	Remedy
Neus	Catalonia	Snow
Ladislav	Croatia	Glorious ruler
Ljubo	Croatia	Peace and love
Velibor	Croatia	Tall pine
Vinko	Latvia	Winning, conqueror
Laco	Czech Republic	Famous ruler
Marika	Czech Republic	Star, sea, may be bitter
Nedda	Czech Republic	Born on Sunday
Ruzena	Czech Republic	Rose
Tepana	Czech Republic	Crowned or crown of laurels
Verka	Czech Republic	Faith of Truth
Vladislava	Czechoslovakia	Glorious ruler
Adolf	Denmark	Noble wolf
Alberth	Denmark	Noble, bright
Alexander	Denmark	Defending men
Alf	Denmark	Elf
Ansgar	Denmark	Spear of God
Arne	Denmark	Eagle

BABY NAMES	COUNTRY	MEANING
Asger	Denmark	Spear of God
Birger	Denmark	Rescue
Bo	Denmark	To live
Dagfinn	Denmark	Day person
Ebbe	Denmark	Wild boar
Egil	Denmark	Terror
Einar	Denmark	One warrior
Emil	Denmark	Rival
Emma	Denmark	Universal
Erland	Denmark	Foreigner
Erling	Denmark	Prince or noble
Folke	Denmark	People
Frode	Denmark	Learned, wise
Svend	Denmark	Young man
Beata	Denmark	Blessed
Bodil	Denmark	Battle remedy
Borghild	Denmark	Battle fortification
Cecilia	Denmark	Blind
Dorothea	Denmark	Gift of God
Edith	Denmark	Wealth and war
Embla	Denmark	Elm
Frida	Denmark	Peace
Gerd	Denmark	Enclosure

BABY NAMES	COUNTRY	MEANING
Aase	Denmark	Tree-covered mountain
Saffi	Denmark	Wisdom
Saffir	Denmark	Sapphire
Semine	Denmark	Goddess of moon, sun and stars
Aart	England	Noble, courageous
Ackerley	England	Meadow of oak trees
Aiken	England	Made of oak
Albert	England	Noble
Aldrich	England	Wise counselor
Aldwin	England	Old friend
Alford	England	Old river ford
Algernon	England	Bearded, wearing a moustache
Alton	England	Town at the source of the river
Asher	England	Happy or blessed
Badrick	England	Axe ruler
Beamer	England	Trumpet player
Blaze	England	Flame
Burnett	England	Brown
Burton	England	Fortified town
Carter	England	Cart driver
Cedric	England	Battle chieftain
Cody	England	Cushions, helpful

BABY NAMES	COUNTRY	MEANING
Colby	England	Dark-haired, coal
Cooper	England	Barrel maker
Cramer	England	To squeeze
Darvell	England	Eagle town
Drake	England	Dragon
Edgar	England	Successful spearman
Edmund	England	Prosperous protector
Edward	England	Prosperous guardian
Elton	England	Old town
Ernest	England	Sincere
Erwin	England	Army/ friend
Farley	England	Bull or sheep meadow
Franklin	England	Free landowner, freeman
Garvin	England	Comrade in battle
Gerard	England	Brave spearman
Hadden	England	From the Moor
Haddon	England	From the heath
Hadon	England	From the heath
Hadrian	England	From Hadria
Hadwin	England	Friend in war
Hadwyn	England	Friend in war
Haefen	England	Safety, refuge, harbor
Haele	England	Lives in the hall

BABY NAMES	COUNTRY	MEANING
Hastings	England	Violent
Haethowine	England	War friend
Hagaleah	England	From the hedged meadow
Hagalean	England	From the hedged enclosure
Hagaward	England	Keeper of the hedged enclosure
Hagley	England	From the hedged enclosure
Hahn	England	Rooster modest
Idal	England	From the yew tree
Iddawg	England	Legendary son of Anarawd
Iddig	England	Thirst
Ifor	England	Lord
Ignatius	England	Fire
Lach	England	Lives near water
Lache	England	Lives near water
Lachimo	England	Cymbeline an Italian
Lad	England	Attendant
Ladbrop	England	Lives by the path
Ladd	England	Attendant
Ladde	England	Attendant
Laddie	England	Attendant
Laec	England	Lives near water

BABY NAMES	COUNTRY	MEANING
Laefertun	England	From the rush farm
Lafeu	England	All well that ends well
Laibrook	England	Lives by the path
Laidley	England	From the creek meadow
Laidly	England	From the creek meadow
Langley	England	Residence name
Lau	England	Welsh form of Zeus life
Leax	England	Salmon
Lke	England	Derived from Hebrew Isaac
Macnair	England	Son of the heir
Newton	England	New town
Nygel	England	Champion from the Irish and Scottish Niall
Palmere	England	Pilgrim
Pelton	England	Town by the lake
Pendragon	England	From the dragons' enclosed land
Perry	England	Rock
Quincey	England	Fifth
Radcliffe	England	Residence
Radolph	England	Red wolf
Raff	England	Red wolf
Ralph	England	Wolf counselor

BABY NAMES	COUNTRY	MEANING
Randy	England	Son of Rand
Ray	England	Wise protector
Rayce	England	Counselor
Reeves	England	Steward
Remington	England	Town of raven
Safford	England	From the willow ford
Scott	England	From Scotland
Seldon	England	From the willow valley
Selwin	England	Friend at court
Sheree	England	Dear or dearest
Sherlock	England	Fair-haired
Sherwin	England	Eminent in friendship
Skeet	England	Swift
Starla	England	Bright star
Storme	England	Tempest
Sylvester	England	From the forest or woods
Tayler	England	Tailor
Todd	England	Fox
Tyla	England	good
Udell	England	Grove of trees
Udolf	England	Prosperous wolf
Vale	England	Lives in the valley
Valen	England	Lives in the valley

BABY NAMES	COUNTRY	MEANING
Vinn	England	Conqueror
Vonn	England	Little
Wada	England	Advancer
Wade	England	Cross the river
Wadsworth	England	From Wades estate
Wain	England	Craftsman
Wait	England	guard
Waldo	England	God's power
Warren	England	To preserve
Warrick	England	Strong leader
Warwick	England	Settlement near the weir
Washington	England	Town near the water
Watt	England	Hurdle
Wayne	England	Wagon maker
Webster	England	Weaver
Weiborn	England	From the spring brook
Welby	England	From the spring farm
Wells	England	From the city in England
Whit	England	White
Wynter	England	Born in winter
Zain	England	God is gracious
Zak	England	Remembered by God

BABY NAMES	COUNTRY	MEANING
Zayne	England	God is gracious
Alfreda	England	Wise, elf counselor
Edeline	England	Noble
Felicity	England	Fortunate, happy
Hadleigh	England	Girl in the Heather
Hadu	England	Vigorous battle maiden
Haesel	England	Nut
Hafwen	England	Summer beauty
Idelia	England	bountiful
Idla	England	Battle
Ifig	England	Ivy
Lanie	England	Path
Lyra	England	Musical instrument
Mabyn	England	Forever young
Nancy	England	Gracious
Queen	England	Queen
Ravyn	England	Dark-haired or wise
Rea	England	Brook
Saeran	England	Irish saint
Sebille	England	Fairy
Sheryl	England	Charity
Starlene	England	Star
Synne	England	Gift from the sun

BABY NAMES	COUNTRY	MEANING
Tacey	England	silent
Tina	England	River
Twila	England	Third
Udele	England	Rich or prosperous
Unwine	England	Unfriendly
Vigena	England	Virginal, chaste
Wann	England	Pale
Wareine	England	Gamekeeper
Zadie	England	Princess
Zerenity	England	Serene, calm
Billie	England	Strong-willed
Blythe	England	Carefree, merry
Breeze	England	Light wind, carefree
Lane	England	Narrow road
Alden	England	Old, wise protector
Blade	England	Knife, sword
Blake	England	Attractive, dark
Iden	England	Prosperous
Palmer	England	Palm bearer
Penn	England	Corral
Perri	England	Wanderer
Peyton	England	village
Piper	England	Flute player

BABY NAMES	COUNTRY	MEANING
Raleigh	England	Field of the birds
Raven	England	Black bird
Reed	England	A reed or red-haired
Stacy	England	Resurrection
Taffy	England	Beloved
Taylor	England	Tailor
Thane	England	Warrior
Tyler	England	Tile-maker
Tyme	England	Thyme herb
Vail	England	Valley
Valiant	England	Brave
Vaughn	England	Small
Vian	England	Full of life
Vine	England	Vineyard worker
Whitney	England	White island
Wynn	England	Fair complexion
Yale	England	Mountain goat
Yates	England	Gates
Eikki	Finland	Ever powerful
Talo	Finland	House
Tahti	Finland	Star
Aadi	France	First, the first
Aimon	France	House

BABY NAMES	COUNTRY	MEANING
Alair	France	Joyful
Ariel	France	Lion of God
Beau	France	Handsome
Bertrand	France	Clever
Blaise	France	Lisping
Boniface	France	Good fate
Boyce	France	Wood, forest
Brice	France	Speckled
Casimir	France	Keeping the peace
Chaunce	France	Fortune, a gamble
Clark	France	Cleric, scholar
Corentin	France	Relative or storm
Darcell	France	Dark
Delmar	France	Of the sea
Dieudonne	France	Given by God
Dillon	France	Loyal
Elouan	France	Light
Farand	France	Gray-haired
Florent	France	Flowering
Francois	France	Free
Gaston	France	From Gascony, France
Gilles	France	Shield / Young goat
Ignace	France	Fiery

BABY NAMES	COUNTRY	MEANING
Obert	France	Noble, bright
Percy	France	Pierces
Raimond	France	Wise protector
Ranier	France	Strong counselor
Raoul	France	Wolf counselor
Talbot	France	Reward
Tyce	France	Fiery
Tyson	France	Explosive
Vachel	France	Small cow
Vallois	France	A Welsh man
Vardan	France	From the green hill
Vardon	France	From the green hill
Vern	France	Youthful, young at heart
Vernay	France	Springlike
Vick	France	Conqueror
Yves	France	Archer
Avril	France	Born on April
Benjamin	France	Son of the South
Blanche	France	White, fair
Cerise	France	Cherry
Coralie	France	Coral
Cosette	France	Little thing
Damica	France	Friendly

BABY NAMES	COUNTRY	MEANING
Darlene	France	Little darling
Dior	France	Golden
Eglantine	France	Botanical name (for the plant sweetbrier)
Emma	France	Whole or universal
Estelle	France	Star
Lacee	France	Derived from Lacey
Lacene	France	Born in the Spring
Laci	France	Derived from lacey
Laciann	France	Derived from lacey
Lacie	France	Derived from lacey
Lacina	France	Derived from Lacey
Lacy	France	From the name Larissa
Lacyann	France	Derived from lacey
La-Vergne	France	Born in the Spring
Laverne	France	Born in the Spring
Marbelle	France	Lovable
Madolen	France	Tower
Michelle	France	Like god
Natalee	France	Birthday
Odelette	France	Wealthy
Paget	France	Assistant
Simone	France	Heard
Solaine	France	Dignified

BABY NAMES	COUNTRY	MEANING
Soleil	France	Sun
Suzette	France	Little lily
Taylar	France	An angel
Valentine	France	Health or love
Valerie	France	Fierce one
Victorina	France	Victory
Vignette	France	Little vine
Vilissa	France	To love and to cherish
Violette	France	Little violet
Ynez	France	Chaste
Ysabel	France	Devoted to God
Amber	France	Amber
Bellamy	France	Beautiful friend
Marvel	France	Miracle
Paris	France	Downfall
Remy	France	From Rheims
Talen	France	Claw
Urbain	France	From the urban
Val	France	Power
Adelard	Germany	Noble and courageous
Adler	Germany	Eagle
Adolf	Germany	Noble wolf
Alaric	Germany	Ruler of all

BABY NAMES	COUNTRY	MEANING
Alger	Germany	Noble spearman
Algis	Germany	Spear
Archibald	Germany	Bold
Arnold	Germany	Eagle ruler
Baldric	Germany	Brave ruler
Banett	Germany	Strong as bear
Bernstein	Germany	Amber stone
Bruno	Germany	Brown-haired
Clovis	Germany	Famous soldier
Dino	Germany	Little sword
Emmett	Germany	Industrious, strong
Gary	Germany	Mighty spearman
Gerald	Germany	Mighty spearman
Ibsen	Germany	Archer's son
Ivo	Germany	Yew wood
Lance	Germany	Spear
Meinard	Germany	Firm
Nikolaus	Germany	Victorious
Pepin	Germany	Determined
Rafael	Germany	God heals
Reginald	Germany	Adviser of the king
Rei	Germany	Mighty or intelligent
Siegfried	Germany	victorious

BABY NAMES	COUNTRY	MEANING
Ubel	Germany	Evil
Ulises	Germany	Noble leader
Ulrich	Germany	Noble leader
Utz	Germany	Ruler
Uwe	Germany	Universal ruler
Valdis	Germany	Spirited in war
Wagner	Germany	Wagon maker
Walter	Germany	Army general
Wesley	Germany	The west meadow
Xiomar	Germany	Famous in battle
Yohann	Germany	God is gracious
Ada	Germany	Prosperous, happy
Adelaide	Germany	Noble and serene
Alarice	Germany	Ruler of all
Alberta	Germany	Noble and bright
Alfonsa	Germany	Noble and eager
Anselma	Germany	Protection
Armine	Germany	Soldier
Arnelle	Germany	Eagle
Bathilda	Germany	Warrior
Berdine	Germany	Glorious, inner light
Berdine	Germany	Glorious, inner light
Brunhilda	Germany	Armored soldier

BABY NAMES	COUNTRY	MEANING
Dagmar	Germany	Glorious
Fulla	Germany	Full
Haduwin	Germany	Strife
Hadwig	Germany	Refuge from battle
Hailey	Germany	Hero
Ida	Germany	Hardworking
Idaia	Germany	Active
Idalie	Germany	Active
Idalina	Germany	Working noble
Idaline	Germany	Working noble
Idelia	Germany	Bountiful
Idetta	Germany	hardworking
Idette	Germany	hardworking
Idna	Germany	Active
Idone	Germany	Hardworking
Idonia	Germany	Industrious
Matilda	Germany	Powerful Battler
Oda	Germany	Elfin spear
Susanne	Germany	Lily
Uda	Germany	Prosperous, rich
Uli	Germany	Mistress of all
Ulrika	Germany	Universal ruler
Vala	Germany	Singled out

BABY NAMES	COUNTRY	MEANING
Vanda	Germany	Wanderer
Verena	Germany	Protector
Vidis	Germany	Holy spirit of the forest
Walda	Germany	Ruler
Wanda	Germany	Slender, young tree
Welda	Germany	Ruler
Zelda	Germany	Woman warrior
Aubrey	Germany	Noble
Mandell	Germany	Almond
Obert	Germany	Wealthy
Porsche	Germany	Offering
Tanner	Germany	Leather worker
Ulf	Germany	Wolf
Adonis	Greece	Highly attractive
Adrian	Greece	Rich
Aeneas	Greece	Praised
Agamemnon	Greece	Resolute
Akakios	Greece	Innocent, not evil
Alcandor	Greece	Manly, strong
Altair	Greece	Star
Anargyros	Greece	Poor, incorruptible
Anastasius	Greece	Resurrection
Argyris	Greece	Silver

BABY NAMES	COUNTRY	MEANING
Arion	Greece	Enchanted
Aristides	Greece	Son of the best
Aristotle	Greece	Best, wise
Athanasios	Greece	Immortal
Castor	Greece	Beaver
Charalampos	Greece	To shine from happiness
Chrysander	Greece	Golden
Chrysanthos	Greece	Golden flower
Cleon	Greece	Famous
Cornelius	Greece	Cornel tree
Corydon	Greece	Helmet, crest
Damon	Greece	Constant, loyal
Demetrius	Greece	Lover of the earth
Elias	Greece	The Lord is my God
Eugene	Greece	Born to nobility
Evander	Greece	Benevolent ruler
George	Greece	Farmer
Gorgios	Greece	Farmer
Haemon	Greece	Son of Creon
Ibycus	Greece	A bard
Icarus	Greece	Son of Daedalus
Icelos	Greece	Son of Hypnos
Idas	Greece	An Argonaut

BABY NAMES	COUNTRY	MEANING
Idomeneus	Greece	A king of Crete
Igorr	Greece	Farmer
Ladon	Greece	Dragon of Hera
Laertes	Greece	Father of Odysseus
Lapetus	Greece	A titan
Lasion	Greece	Father of Plutus
Lason	Greece	Healer
Leksi	Greece	Defender of men
Lestrygones	Greece	The tribe of giants
Odysseus	Greece	Full of wrath
Otis	Greece	One who hears well
Pan	Greece	God of flocks
Panagiotis	Greece	All holy
Panchito	Greece	Free
Pancho	Greece	Plume
Pandarus	Greece	Killed for breaking a truce
Pander	Greece	A pimp
Pascual	Greece	Passover
Pelias	Greece	Son of Poseidon
Pheobus	Greece	Shining
Phil	Greece	Lover of Horses
Photios	Greece	Light
Priam	Greece	King of Troy

BABY NAMES	COUNTRY	MEANING
Rasmus	Greece	Amiable
Sirius	Greece	Dog star
Sotiris	Greece	Salvation
Than	Greece	Death, brilliant
Thaumas	Greece	Father of the harpies
Theo	Greece	Gift
Timothy	Greece	To honor God
Tymon	Greece	Praise the Lord
Urian	Greece	From heaven
Vaseleios	Greece	Regal
Xanthus	Greece	Blond
Xeno	Greece	Strange voice
Yehor	Greece	Farmer
Yurii	Greece	Farmer
Acacia	Greece	Thorny
Achima	Greece	Jehovah raises up
Adara	Greece	Beauty
Adelfa/ Adelpha	Greece	Born of the same womb, sister
Adelpha	Greece	Sister
Adonia	Greece	My Lord
Agatha	Greece	Good, kind
Aglaia	Greece	Beautiful
Agnes	Greece	Pure

BABY NAMES	COUNTRY	MEANING
Aikaterine	Greece	Each of the two
Alcina	Greece	Strong-minded
Alexa	Greece	Defender of mankind
Alice	Greece	Truthful
Angeliki	Greece	Angelic
Azalea	Greece	Dry
Calandra	Greece	Lark
Calliope	Greece	Beautiful voice
Calypso	Greece	Concealer
Chara	Greece	Happiness, joy
Damara	Greece	Gentle girl
Daryn	Greece	Gifts
Despoina	Greece	Mistress, lady
Dessa	Greece	Wanderer
Diamanto	Greece	Diamond
Diantha	Greece	Divine flower
Dimitra	Greece	Earth Mother
Dionne	Greece	Divine queen
Doris	Greece	Sea
Eleanor	Greece	Light
Electra	Greece	Shining, brilliant
Evangeline	Greece	Bearer of good news
Fotina	Greece	Light

BABY NAMES	COUNTRY	MEANING
Hailie	Greece	Hero
Ica	Greece	Light
Idoia	Greece	Vision
Idylla	Greece	Perfect
Lachesis	Greece	A fate
Lanthe	Greece	Violet flower
Lanthina	Greece	Flower
Lasius	Greece	Mother of Atlanta
Liithya	Greece	Goddess of woman in labor
Melina	Greece	Honey
Nell	Greece	Stone
Nympha	Greece	Bride
Oleander	Greece	Evergreen
Ophelia	Greece	Helper
Pam	Greece	Honey
Pam	Greece	Honey
Pamela	Greece	Honey
Pamelia	Greece	Covered with Honey
Panagiota	Greece	All holy
Panagiotis	Greece	All Holy
Pandora	Greece	Gifted
Pansy	Greece	A thought
Penelope	Greece	Dream weaver

BABY NAMES	COUNTRY	MEANING
Penney	Greece	Silent worker
Peri	Greece	Lives in the mountains
Phedora	Greece	Supreme gift
Pheobe	Greece	Sparkling
Psyche	Greece	Soul
Reit	Greece	Speaker
Saina	Greece	Princess
Sandie	Greece	Protector and helper
Sandra	Greece	Helper of humanity
Santos	Greece	Saint
Sapphire	Greece	Sapphire gemstone
Scylla	Greece	Sea monster
Selene	Greece	Moon
Selina	Greece	Moon
Sirena	Greece	Siren
Stacey	Greece	Resurrection
Sybil	Greece	Prophet
Sybyl	Greece	Oracle
Tasha	Greece	Born on Christmas
Tryn	Greece	Innocent
Urania	Greece	Heavenly
Vanessa	Greece	Butterfly
Vangie	Greece	Bringer of good news

BABY NAMES	COUNTRY	MEANING
Venus	Greece	Goddess of beauty
Veronika	Greece	Honest image
Vilmaris	Greece	Protector of the sea
Xenia	Greece	Foreigner, guest
Xylina	Greece	Of the woods
Yalena	Greece	Light
Zandra	Greece	Defender of all
Zebina	Greece	One who is gifted
Zoe	Greece	Life
Zosima	Greece	lively
Carey	Greece	Pure
Cyril	Greece	Lordly
Drew	Greece	Courageous, strong
Lyric	Greece	Melodic word
Myles	Greece	Soldier
Pallas	Greece	Wisdom
Salus	Greece	Goddess of health
Tynan	Greece	Dark
Xylon	Greece	Lives in the forest
Zale	Greece	Sea strength
Zephyr	Greece	Gentle wind
Ince	Hungary	Innocent
Marton	Hungary	Warriors of mars

BABY NAMES	COUNTRY	MEANING
Samuka	Hungary	God hears
Soma	Hungary	Horn
Tamas	Hungary	Twin
Vencel	Hungary	Victorious
Ibolya	Hungary	Violet
Sasa	Hungary	Princess
Viva	Hungary	Life
Aidan	Ireland	Fiery
Alan	Ireland	Handsome, peaceful
Alpin	Ireland	Attractive
Bowie	Ireland	Yellow-haired
Cavan	Ireland	Handsome
Cian	Ireland	Ancient
Ciaran	Ireland	Black, little
Colin	Ireland	Young cub
Conan	Ireland	Praised, exalted
Crevan	Ireland	Fox
Cullen	Ireland	Handsome
Darcy	Ireland	Dark
Delaney	Ireland	Descendant of the challenger
Dempsey	Ireland	Proud
Doherty	Ireland	Harmful
Evan	Ireland	Young warrior

BABY NAMES	COUNTRY	MEANING
Finian	Ireland	Light-skinned
Gair	Ireland	Small
Idwal	Ireland	The lord of the wall
Ighnwachan	Ireland	Derived from Eigneachan
Lain	Ireland	God is gracious
Laird	Ireland	Head of Household
Lan	Ireland	God is gracious
Lestin	Ireland	Just or true
Lestyn	Ireland	God is gracious
Leuan	Ireland	God is gracious
Nally	Ireland	Poor
Neil	Ireland	Champion
Patrick	Ireland	Nobleman
Penrose	Ireland	End or top of the moor
Sweeney	Ireland	Little hero
Troy	Ireland	Water or foot soldier
Wallace	Ireland	Stranger
Acima	Ireland	Praised by God
Africa	Ireland	Pleasant
Airlea	Ireland	Promise
Airleas	Ireland	Promise
Alana	Ireland	Attractive, peaceful
Alanis	Ireland	Beautiful, bright

BABY NAMES	COUNTRY	MEANING
Arlene	Ireland	Pledge
Artis	Ireland	Noble
Barie	Ireland	Spear, markswoman
Breena	Ireland	Fairy palace
Brenda	Ireland	Little raven
Branna	Ireland	Little raven
Briana	Ireland	Strong, virtuous
Bridget	Ireland	Strong
Caitlin	Ireland	Pure
Cara	Ireland	Friend
Catriona	Ireland	Clear, pure
Deirdre	Ireland	Sorrowful, wanderer
Derry	Ireland	Redhead
Earlene	Ireland	Pledge
Ibernia	Ireland	From Ireland
Ide	Ireland	Noble
Idelisa	Ireland	bountiful
Labhaoise	Ireland	Warrior Maiden
Lace	Ireland	Warrior Maiden
Laetitia	Ireland	Irish form of Letitia
Lanna	Ireland	Female for of Ian
Lerne	Ireland	From Ireland
Mabina	Ireland	Nimble

BABY NAMES	COUNTRY	MEANING
Makayla	Ireland	Like a god
Megan	Ireland	Soft and gentle
Shiela	Ireland	Blind
Siobahn	Ireland	God is gracious
Tara	Ireland	Tower, hillside
Ula	Ireland	Jewel of the sea
Uny	Ireland	Together
Vevina	Ireland	Sweet lady
Zaira	Ireland	Princess
Blaine	Ireland	Thin
Brady	Ireland	Spirited
Breck	Ireland	Freckled
Brogan	Ireland	A heavy work shoe
Dallas	Ireland	Wise
Enda	Ireland	Bird
Hadley	Ireland	Heath near the wasteland
Hagan	Ireland	Ruler of the home
Hagen	Ireland	Little, young
Lachlan	Ireland	From the lake
Maeron	Ireland	Bitter
Mel	Ireland	Mill workers
Quillan	Ireland	Cub
Quinn	Ireland	Fifth

BABY NAMES	COUNTRY	MEANING
Reagan	Ireland	Son of the ruler
Ryan	Ireland	Young royalty
Sean	Ireland	God is gracious
Shane	Ireland	God is gracious
Skye	Ireland	From the isle of Skye
Taban	Ireland	Genius
Abrial	Italy	Open, secure, protected
Ace	Italy	Unity
Agapito	Italy	Beloved
Albion	Italy	White cliffs
Aldo	Italy	Old, elder
Aleron	Italy	Winged
Alessandro	Italy	Defending men
Alfonso	Italy	Noble and ready
Amadeus	Italy	Loves God
Andrea	Italy	Strong, courageous
Camilo	Italy	Child born to freedom
Curtis	Italy	Enclosure
Devine	Italy	Divine
Errol	Italy	Wanderer
Fabian	Italy	Bean grower
Faust	Italy	Lucky, fortunate
Francesco	Italy	Free one

BABY NAMES	COUNTRY	MEANING
Gabriel	Italy	Devoted to God
Leonardo	Italy	Brave Lion
Lorenzo	Italy	From Larentum
Mattea	Italy	Gift of God
Matteo	Italy	Gift of God
Maurizio	Italy	Dark-skinned, moor
Paolo	Italy	Little
Placido	Italy	Calm, quiet
Primo	Italy	First born
Ricardo	Italy	Firm ruler
Tino	Italy	Small
Ugo	Italy	Intelligence, wit
Uso	Italy	Intelligent
Vito	Italy	Life
Adawna	Italy	Beautiful sunrise
Adelaide	Italy	Noble
Adora	Italy	Beloved
Adrienna	Italy	Dark or rich
Agrippina	Italy	Born feet first
Alice	Italy	Truthful
Aurora	Italy	dawn
Bambi	Italy	Child
Chiara	Italy	Clear and bright

BABY NAMES	COUNTRY	MEANING
Emma	Italy	Flatterer
Gaia	Italy	Earth
Giukia	Italy	Youthful
Goergia	Italy	Farmer, art
Lanza	Italy	Noble and eager
Mariabella	Italy	A beautiful Mary
Martina	Italy	Martial, water-like
Nicci	Italy	Victory
Patrizia	Italy	Noble
Sara	Italy	Princess
Siena	Italy	City of Tuscany
Sienna	Italy	Dark brown
Sofia	Italy	Wise
Valeria	Italy	Strength, valor
Venitia	Italy	Mercy
Vita	Italy	Life
Volante	Italy	Flying
Carina	Italy	Dear little one
Celestine	Italy	Heavenly
Quorra	Italy	Heart
Sabin	Italy	From the Sabines
Aage	Norway	Ancestors
Aksel	Norway	Father of peace

BABY NAMES	COUNTRY	MEANING
Haaken	Norway	Of the way
Hafgrim	Norway	A settler of Greenland
Hafleikr	Norway	Sea war
Hafnar	Norway	Help, save, rescue
Lagmann	Norway	Lawyer
Olivir	Norway	Affectionate
Skipp	Norway	Ship owner
Svan	Norway	Swan
Tajei	Norway	Spear of Thor
Ymir	Norway	A mythical giant
Elga	Norway	Pious
Idona	Norway	Norse goddess
Idun	Norway	Active in love
Iduna	Norway	Active in love
Ranveig	Norway	House woman
Sigrid	Norway	A beautiful victory
Sigrun	Norway	Secret victory
Skade	Norway	Goddess of skiers
Svenhilda	Norway	Swan or warrior
Syn	Norway	Invoked during trials
Unni	Norway	Modest
Valda	Norway	Spirited warrior
Volva	Norway	Prophetess

BABY NAMES	COUNTRY	MEANING
Yulene	Norway	Born during Yule
Bodil	Norway	Mighty ruler
Bronislaw	Poland	Weapon of glory
Cerek	Poland	Lordly
Rasine	Poland	Rose
Ramiro	Portugal	Supreme judge
Xanti	Portugal	Name of St. James
Yelena	Portugal	Light
Igoryok	Russian	Farmer
Sasha	Russian	Helper and protector
Urie	Russian	God is light
Vadim	Russian	Powerful ruler
Vas	Russian	Royal
Vassily	Russian	Royal
Vladimir	Russian	Has peace
Yevgeni	Russian	The noble
Yurik	R u s s i a (Male)	Farmer
Zenaida	Russia	From Zeus
Alena	Russia	Light
Larisa	Russia	Citadel
Lyubov	Russia	Love
Nadya	Russia	Hope
Raisa	Russia	Rose

BABY NAMES	COUNTRY	MEANING
Sanvi	Russia	Knowledge
Sanya	Russia	To dream
Sinovia	Russia	Stranger
Varinka	Russia	Stranger
Veda	Russia	Knowledge, understanding
Vilma	Russia	Resolute protector
Zasha	Russia	People's defender
Aaren	Scandinavia	Lofty or inspired
Bjorg	Scandinavia	Salvation
Borg	Scandinavia	Castle
Bragi	Scandinavia	Poet
Elvis	Scandinavia	Wise
Eric	Scandinavia	Ruler of all
Garth	Scandinavia	Garden, gardener
Gudbrand	Scandinavia	Sword of God
Gudmund	Scandinavia	God's Protection
Gunnar	Scandinavia	Warrior
Gustav	Scandinavia	Goth staff
Halden	Scandinavia	Half- Danish
Hamar	Scandinavia	Hammer
Helge	Scandinavia	Blessed, holy
Hemming	Scandinavia	Shape
Herman	Scandinavia	Army man

BABY NAMES	COUNTRY	MEANING
Hjalmar	Scandinavia	Warrior's helmet
Igor	Scandinavia	Heroic warrior
Lamonte	Scandinavia	Man of Law
Olaf	Scandinavia	Ancestor
Osbourne	Scandinavia	Born from a bear
Oscar	Scandinavia	Accurate spearman
Rydell	Scandinavia	Horseman, rider
Svein	Scandinavia	Youthful, young at heart
Thor	Scandinavia	Thunder
Astrid	Scandinavia	Divine strength
Freya	Scandinavia	Noblewoman
Gudrun	Scandinavia	God's secret lore
Gunda	Scandinavia	War
Gunhild	Scandinavia	Battle
Gunvor	Scandinavia	Vigilant warrior
Hilda	Scandinavia	Battle
Hildegard	Scandinavia	Battle enclosure
Inca	Scandinavia	Ing's abundance
Laine	Scandinavia	Waves
Satu	Scandinavia	Fairytale
Siv	Scandinavia	Kinship
Swann	Scandinavia	Swan-like
Tyra	Scandinavia	Goddess of battle

BABY NAMES	COUNTRY	MEANING
Ursa	Scandinavia	Bear
Ursula	Scandinavia	Female bear
Maj	Scandinavia	A pearl
Uther	Scotland	Arthur's father
Ahearn	Scotland	Lord of the horses
Artis	Scotland	Bear
Calan	Scotland	Victorious people
Chalmers	Scotland	Son of the lord
Connor	Scotland	Wise
Labhruinn	Scotland	Laurel
Lachie	Scotland	The boy from the lochs
Lachlann	Scotland	From Scandinavia
Lagan	Scotland	The little fiery one
Lailoken	Scotland	A fool
Paismedes	Scotland	A knight
Palomydes	Scotland	A knight
Ramsay	Scotland	Island of rams
Taggart	Scotland	Pastor's son
Uriens	Scotland	Name of kings
Aileen	Scotland	Light bearer
Ailsa	Scotland	Island dweller
Ailsa	Scotland	Island dweller
Alastrina	Scotland	Defender of humankind

BABY NAMES	COUNTRY	MEANING
Iblis	Scotland	Wife of Lancelot
Idelle	Scotland	bountiful
Igerne	Scotland	Mother of Arthur
Ingraine	Scotland	Mother of Arthur
Isobel	Scotland	Consecrated to God
Jean	Scotland	God is gracious
Lainie	Scotland	Serves John
Lair	Scotland	Male
Maegan	Scotland	Pearl
Nairna	Scotland	Dwells at the alder tree
Nineve	Scotland	Lady of the lake
Talwyn	Scotland	A fair brow
Vika	Scotland	From the creek
Ygraine	Scotland	Mother of Arthur
Ainsley	Scotland	My own meadow
Berkley	Scotland	Birch tree meadow
Blair	Scotland	Plain dweller
Bonny	Scotland	Pretty
Camden	Scotland	Winding valley
Tait	Scotland	Cheerful
Lacko	Slovakia	Famous ruler
Ladislas	Slovakia	Good ruler
Ladislav	Slovakia	A glorious ruler

BABY NAMES	COUNTRY	MEANING
Lel	Slovakia	Taker
Sagan	Slovakia	Wise one
Vlad	Slovakia	Prince
Idania	Slovakia	Hardworking, prosperous
Lada	Slovakia	Goddess of love and fertility
Olga	Slovakia	Holy
Radinka	Slovakia	Joyful
Sonia	Slovakia	Wisdom
Stacia	Slovakia	Resurrection
Sveta	Slovakia	Bright light
Tana	Slovakia	Fairy queen
Tania	Slovakia	Fairy queen
Tatiana	Slovakia	Fairy queen
Yanka	Slovakia	God is good
Vanya	Slovakia	Gracious
Ignacio	Spain	Fire
Ibon	Spain	archer
Alroy	Spain	King
Alvaro	Spain	Just, wise
Bertin	Spain	Distinguished friend
Blanco	Spain	Light-skinned
Cid	Spain	Lord

BABY NAMES	COUNTRY	MEANING
Domingo	Spain	Born on Sunday
Ignacia	Spain	fire
Ignado	Spain	Fire
Ignazio	Spain	Fire
Liari	Spain	Cheerful
Liian	Spain	youth
Pepe	Spain	He shall add
Raul	Spain	Wolf counselor
Salbatore	Spain	Savior
Segundo	Spain	Born second
Stefano	Spain	Crown of laurels
Tadeo	Spain	Praise
Vicente	Spain	Conquering
Victoriano	Spain	Victorious
Xavier	Spain	New house
Tobie	Sweden	God is good
Adonia	Spain	Beautiful
Alegria	Spain	Cheerful
Belinda	Spain	Beautiful
Bonita	Spain	Pretty
Damita	Spain	Small noblewoman
Esperanza	Spain	Hope
Idurre	Spain	Reference to the virgin

BABY NAMES	COUNTRY	MEANING
Igone	Spain	Male
Itsel	Spain	Shadow
Jadie	Spain	Jade
Jaira	Spain	Jehovah Teacher
Javiera	Spain	Owner of new home
Labonita	Spain	Beautiful One
La-Cienega	Spain	The swamp mashes
Ladonna	Spain	The woman
La-Reina	Spain	Queen
Palma	Spain	Palm
Palmera	Spain	From the city of Palm
Paloma	Spain	A dove
Paquita	Spain	Free
Raina	Spain	Queen, peaceful
Raquel	Spain	Ewe
Reia	Spain	Queen
Sancha	Spain	Holy
Sanita	Spain	Little healthy girl
Savannah	Spain	Open plain, field
Seina	Spain	Innocent
Senona	Spain	Lively
Sierra	Spain	Mountain
Taffia	Spain	An angel's new love

BABY NAMES	COUNTRY	MEANING
Tea	Spain	Princess or aunt
Teresa	Spain	Harvester
Ventura	Spain	Good fortune
Verda	Spain	Truth
Vicenta	Spain	Victorious
Yadra	Spain	Mother
Ynez	Spain	Pure, chaste
Yoana	Spain	God's gift
Ysobel	Spain	Consecrated to God
Zanita	Spain	God's gift
Jayde	Spain	Wise
Palmiera	Spain	Palm Tree
Paz	Spain	Peace or gold
Britta	Sweden	Strong
Lage	Sweden	From the sea
Burian	Ukraine	Lives near weeds
Stanislav	Ukraine	Stand, become
Dewey	Wales	Prized
Gavin	Wales	White hawk
Gerwin	Wales	Fair love
Aerona	Wales	Berry
Bevanne	Wales	Child of Evan
Bevanne	Wales	Child of Evan

BABY NAMES	COUNTRY	MEANING
Blodwyn	Wales	White flower
Bronwen	Wales	White breasted
Caron	Wales	Loving, kind-hearted
Carys	Wales	Love
Eirlys	Wales	Snow drop
Jennifer	Wales	White wave
Brynn	Wales	Mound
Caron	Wales	To love
Eirian	Wales	Bright, beautiful
Glaw	Wales	Rain
Gwynedd	Wales	Ancient Kingdom

2. AFRICA

BABY NAMES	COUNTRY	MEANING
Abasi	Africa	Stern
Abdi	Africa	My servant
Abidemi	Africa	Born during father's absence
Abioye	Africa	Born into royalty
Adebayo	Africa	Crown meets joy
Adisa	Africa	One who is clear
Afi	Africa	Born on Friday
Aframi	Africa	River in Ghana
Ahmed	Africa	Praiseworthy
Ashanti	Africa	Tribe in West Africa
Ashton	Africa	Ash Tree Settlement
Ashur	Africa	Principal Assyrian Deity
Atira	Africa	Gift
Atoofa	Africa	Kind, merciful
Attar	Africa	Perfumer
Atuf	Africa	Affectionate
Atufa	Africa	Kind, Merciful
Atun	Africa	Educator
Audi	Africa	Last Daughter
Auj	Africa	Zenith, climax

BABY NAMES	COUNTRY	MEANING
Aukeilia	Africa	Beautiful Flower
Aun	Africa	Help, Assistance
Aus	Africa	To give gift
Autena	Africa	Go hears me
Avery	Africa	Strong, wise, desired one
Azzam	Africa	Determined
Babafemi	Africa	My father loves me
Bahili	Africa	Inner thoughts
Bakari	Africa	Of noble promise
Baruti	Africa	Teacher
Bem	Africa	Peace
Bobo	Africa	Born on Tuesday
Chane	Africa	Dependable
Chui	Africa	Leopard
Chuma	Africa	Iron, wealthy
Dawd	Africa	Beloved
Enzi	Africa	Powerful
Haji	Africa	Born during the pilgrimage to Mecca
Hamise	Africa	Variant of Haji
Hamisie	Africa	Variant of Haji
Hamisy	Africa	Variant of Haji
Hasani	Africa	Handsome
Abena	Africa	Born on Tuesday

BABY NAMES	COUNTRY	MEANING
Abeni	Africa	We asked for her
Aberash	Africa	Giving off light
Adaeze	Africa	King's daughter
Adanna	Africa	My father's daughter
Adannaya	Africa	Her father's daughter
Aiesha	Africa	Life
Baako	Africa	First Born
Baba	Africa	Born on Thursday
Baderinwa	Africa	Worthy of respect
Badru	Africa	Born between full moons
Bahati	Africa	My luck is good
Barika	Africa	Successful
Bayo	Africa	Joy is found
Bejide	Africa	Born during a rainy season
Bolade	Africa	Honor arrives
Bolanile	Africa	Wealth of his house
Eshe	Africa	Life
Hadiya	Africa	Gift
Hasana	Africa	She arrived first
Hasina	Africa	Good
Hassina	Africa	Good
Huseina	Africa	She arrived first
Jaha	Africa	Dignified

BABY NAMES	COUNTRY	MEANING
Jahaira	Africa	Dignified
Kaluluwa	Africa	Forgotten
Kanene	Africa	A little important thing
Kesi	Africa	Born during difficult times
Kesia	Africa	Favorite
Kia	Africa	Season's beginning
Kisha	Africa	Kitten
Kissa	Africa	Born after twins
Kissa	Africa	Kitten
Kwashi	Africa	Born on Sunday
Kwashi	Africa	Born on Sunday
Kwau	Africa	Born on Thursday
Kwau	Africa	Born on Thursday
Kya	Africa	Diamond in the sky
Kya	Africa	Diamond in the sky
Kyah	Africa	Diamond in the sky
Kyah	Africa	Diamond in the sky
Neema	Africa	Born during prosperous t8mes
Paka	Africa	Kitten
Penda	Africa	Loved
Pita	Africa	4th daughter
Poni	Africa	2nd daughter
Ramla	Africa	Fortune teller

BABY NAMES	COUNTRY	MEANING
Rasheda	Africa	Derived from Rashida
Rashida	Africa	Righteous
Raziya	Africa	Agreeable
Sharik	Africa	Child of God
Shatira	Africa	Distinguished
Siti	Africa	Respectful woman
Zuri	Africa	Beautiful
Zuwena	Africa	Good
Abimbola	Africa	Born wealthy
Abiodun	Africa	Born on a festival
Ade	Africa	Crown

3. NORTH AMERICA

BABY NAMES	COUNTRY	MEANING
Aabot	America	Father
Aaron	America	Exalted one
Abel	America	Breath
Abraham	America	Father of Multitudes
Ace	America	Unity
Ackedey	America	Dweller at acre meadow
Ackley	America	Dweller at the oak tree meadow
Adam	America	Red earth
Adamson	America	Son of Adam
Addis	America	Son of Adam
Addison	America	Son of Adam
Addney	America	Lives on the noble's island
Addy	America	Of the earth
Adken	America	Oaken
Adkins	America	Son of Alken
Adkyn	America	Oaken
Adney	America	Lives on the noble's island
Alerio	America	Eagle
Aric	America	Rule with mercy

BABY NAMES	COUNTRY	MEANING
Nahele	America	Forest
Nahios-Si	America	Three fingers
Nahma	America	Sturgeon
Nakos	America	Sage
Nalu	America	Wave
Nantai	America	Chief
Nantan	America	Spokesman
Napayshni	America	Strong
Nash	America	Adventurer
Nashashuk	America	Loud thunder
Nashoba	America	Wolf
Nawat	America	Left handed
Nawkah	America	Wood
Nayati	America	He who wrestles
Neacal	America	He who wrestles
Neka	America	Wild Goose
Ocunnwhurst	America	Yellow wolf
Odakota	America	Friend
Ogima	America	chief
Ohanko	America	Reckless
Ohanzee	America	Shadow
Abedabun	America	Sight of Day

BABY NAMES	COUNTRY	MEANING
Abegail	America	My father rejoices
Abilene	America	A plain
Ada	America	Wealthy
Adaline	America	Noble
Adda	America	Wealthy
Imala	America	Strong-minded
Nachelle	America	Powerful Woman
Nahimana	America	Mystic
Namid	America	Star
Napua	America	The flowers
Nascha	America	Owl
Nashota	America	Twin
Nata	America	Speaker
Natane	America	Female child
Natanie	America	Heaven Come
Naylene	America	Caring
Neena	America	Mighty
Neleh	America	Beautiful light
Nerice	America	Powerful woman
Netanya	America	God's gift
Netis	America	Trustworthy
Nevaeh	America	heaven
Nevaeha	America	Gift from god

BABY NAMES	COUNTRY	MEANING
Obtobre	America	Tenth month
Odahingum	America	Ripping water
Ogin	America	Wild rose
Olathe	America	Lovely
Olina	America	Joyous
Aala	Hawaii	Hunter and healer
Aaralyn	Hawaii	With song
Abegaila	Hawaii	My father is joy
Abequa	Hawaii	Stays at home
Abeque	Hawaii	Stays at home
Hawaiian	Hawaii	Lily
Kalani	Hawaii	Torch
Kalea	Hawaii	Bright, clear
Kalei	Hawaii	Flower wreath
Kalena	Hawaii	Pure
Kaliah	Hawaii	Kaliah
Kalina	Hawaii	Flower
Kameli	Hawaii	Honey
Kanani	Hawaii	Beautiful
Kani	Hawaii	Sound
Kanoa	Hawaii	Free
Kapua	Hawaii	Blossom
Kaylea	Hawaii	Derived from kalea

BABY NAMES	COUNTRY	MEANING
Keala	Hawaii	Path
Keiki	Hawaii	Child
Kilia	Hawaii	Heaven
Kina	Hawaii	From China
Kini	Hawaii	Form of Jean
Kiora	Hawaii	Brown hills
Lea	Hawaii	Goddess of canoe makers
Leilani	Hawaii	Heavenly flower
Lolanah	Hawaii	Soaring like a hawk
Mahina	Hawaii	Moon glow
Makala	Hawaii	A form of Michaela
Makana	Hawaii	Gift, present
Makani	Hawaii	Wind
Malana	Hawaii	Buoyant, light
Maliah	Hawaii	Form of Malia
Maliyah	Hawaii	Malia
Maluhia	Hawaii	Peaceful
Mamo	Hawaii	Saffron flower, yellow bird
Mana	Hawaii	Psychic
Manal	Hawaii	Mana
Mausi	Hawaii	Plucked flower
Mele	Hawaii	Song, poem
Miliani	Hawaii	Caress

BABY NAMES	COUNTRY	MEANING
Moana	Hawaii	Ocean
Mohala	Hawaii	Flowers in bloom
Nalani	Hawaii	Calm as the heavens
Okelani	Hawaii	From Heaven
Pala	Hawaii	Water
Pana	Hawaii	Partridge
Pocahontas	Hawaii	Playful
Pua	Hawaii	Flower
Puakea	Hawaii	White flower
Rapa	Hawaii	Moonbeam
Roselani	Hawaii	Heavenly rose
Sapata	Hawaii	Dancing bear
Satinka	Hawaii	Sacred dancer
Shada	Hawaii	Pelican
Shadia	Hawaii	Form of Shada
Shappa	Hawaii	Red thunder
Shug	Hawaii	Sugar
Sihu	Hawaii	Flower, bush
Sisika	Hawaii	Songbird
Soso	Hawaii	Tree squirrel
Suke	Hawaii	Lily
Sukey	Hawaii	Lily
Suse	Hawaii	Lily

BABY NAMES	COUNTRY	MEANING
Tala	Hawaii	Stalking wolf
Teisha	Hawaii	Joy
Ualani	Hawaii	Rain from heaven
Wainani	Hawaii	Beautiful water
Wila	Hawaii	Loyal, faithful
Wilikinia	Hawaii	A form of Virginia
Wyanet	Hawaii	Legendary beauty
Wyoming	Hawaii	A western state of USA
Yenene	Hawaii	Shaman
Jaden	American	God has heard
Natani	American	Heaven come
Nature	American	Nature
Navid	American	Beloved
Nebraska	American	Flat water
Neo	American	new
Ohio	American	Large river
Rene	American	Reborn

4. SOUTH AMERICA

BABY NAMES	COUNTRY	MEANING
Adelio	Cuba	Noble
Ana	Dominican Republic	Gracious
Alvita	Jamaican	Vivacious
Abantiades	Latin America	Descendant of Abas
Academicus	Latin America	Name of Philosopher
Accius	Latin America	A Roma Poet
Ace	Latin America	Unity, One
Achaean	Latin America	A Greek
Achaemenes	Latin America	A Persian
Achaemenius	Latin America	A Persian
Achaeus	Latin America	A Greek
Achates	Latin America	A friend of Aeneas
Acheros	Latin America	River of Sorrow
Achillides	Latin America	Descendant of Achilles
Achivus	Latin America	A Greek
Acrisionades	Latin America	Descendant of Acrisius
Actaeon	Latin America	A hunter
Actaeonis	Latin America	A Hunter
Actaeus	Latin America	From Athens

BABY NAMES	COUNTRY	MEANING
Actor	Latin America	Son of Azeus
Actoris	Latin America	Son of Azeus
Adok	Latin America	Of the Adriatic
Adolfo	Latin America	Wolf
Adrian	Latin America	Of the Adriatic
Adriano	Latin America	From the Adriatic
Adrik	Latin America	Of the Adriatic
Aegaeus	Latin America	From the Aegean Sea
Aegeus	Latin America	From the Aegean Sea
Aemilianus	Latin America	From the Roman clan name
Aeneades	Latin America	Roman Family clan name
Aeolius	Latin America	Mythical keeper
Aeriona	Latin America	Beauty
Aeriona	Latin America	Beauty
Aeschylus	Latin America	Athenian Poet
Aeslapius	Latin America	God of medicine
Aethiops	Latin America	An Ethiopian
Agosto	Latin America	Derived from August
Agoston	Latin America	Majestic
Agustino	Latin America	Derived from August
Alacibiades	Latin America	Name of an Athenian

BABY NAMES	COUNTRY	MEANING
Alban	Latin America	From the city of alba
Albano	Latin America	White
Alben	Latin America	Fair blond
Albion	Latin America	White or Fair
Alcaeus	Latin America	A Greek poet
Aldnous	Latin America	Father of Nausicaa
Alejandro	Latin America	Defender of Men
Alerio	Latin America	Eagle
Almy	Latin America	Legal
Alver	Latin America	White
Alvern	Latin America	Spring
Amadeo	Latin America	Loves God
Amadeus	Latin America	Love of God
Amadio	Latin America	Loves God
Amaximader	Latin America	Name of a Greek
Amaximenes	Latin America	Greek Philosopher
Amias	Latin America	Loves God
Amyas	Latin America	Loves God
Anacreon	Latin America	Name of an ancient pot
Anawgoras	Latin America	Graced with God's bounty
Ancile	Latin America	King of Rome
Ancyra	Latin America	From Ankara

BABY NAMES	COUNTRY	MEANING
Andrion	Latin America	Of the Adriatic
Angelo	Latin America	Angel
Anguis	Latin America	Dragon
Antal	Latin America	Beyond Praise
Antanas	Latin America	Beyond Praise
Antanelis	Latin America	Beyond Praise
Antenor	Latin America	An elder of Troy
Antisthenes	Latin America	Name of Philosopher
Antoin	Latin America	Beyond Praise
Antonella	Latin America	Praiseworthy
Antonin	Latin America	Beyond praise
Antoniv	Latin America	Beyond Praise
Antony	Latin America	Praise worthy
Antton	Latin America	Beyond Praise
Apollodorus	Latin America	Name of a Greek Writer
Claudio	Latin America	Lame
Clodoveo	Latin America	Famous Warrior
Conrado	Latin America	Able counsel
Constantino	Latin America	Constant
Consuelo	Latin America	Consolation
Cordero	Latin America	Sheep
Cornelio	Latin America	Horn

BABY NAMES	COUNTRY	MEANING
Delmar	Latin America	From the sea
Eduardo	Latin America	Wealthy guard
Elonso	Latin America	Fit for battle
Enrico	Latin America	Ruler of the house
Ernesto	Latin America	Serious-minded
Esteban	Latin America	Man with crown
Everardo	Latin America	Courageous like a boar
Faustino	Latin America	Fortunate
Gonzalo	Latin America	Safe fight
Guillermo	Latin America	Strong mind and protection
Humberto	Latin America	Bright fighter
Aandromacha	Latin America	Wife of Hector
Abril	Latin America	April
Academia	Latin America	Named for Ciceros villa
Acarnania	Latin America	From Acarnania
Acarnanus	Latin America	From Acarnania
Acidalia	Latin America	Named for Venus
Adalira	Latin America	Fairy of the harp
Adora	Latin America	Beloved One
Adorabella	Latin America	Adored beauty
Adoree	Latin America	Glory
Adoria	Latin America	Glory

BABY NAMES	COUNTRY	MEANING
Adrasteia	Latin America	Unyielding
Adrie	Latin America	Of the Adriatic
Aea	Latin America	From Aea
Aegae	Latin America	From the Aegean Sea
Aegates	Latin America	From the Aegates
Aegeria	Latin America	Cumaean
Aegina	Latin America	Mother of Aeacus
Aeginae	Latin America	Mother of Aecacus
Aeolia	Latin America	Daughter of Anythaon
Aggie	Latin America	Lamb
Aggripinae	Latin America	Colonist
Agrafine	Latin America	Born feet first
Agrippina	Latin America	Colonist
Agustina	Latin America	Majestic
Aida	Latin America	Helper
Aida	Latin America	Winged
Alaura	Latin America	From the laurel tree
Albula	Latin America	From the fiber
Alcamene	Latin America	Mother of Hercules
Alcimede	Latin America	Mother of Jason
Alcimena	Latin America	Mother of Hercules
Alcumena	Latin America	Mother of Hercules

BABY NAMES	COUNTRY	MEANING
Aleda	Latin America	Small and winged
Alice	Latin America	Of the nobility
Aleecia	Latin America	Derived from Alice
Aleesha	Latin America	Derived from Alice
Alera	Latin America	Eagle
Aleria	Latin America	Eagle
Alexandrea	Latin America	Defender of Men
Alexandriana	Latin America	Defender of Men
Alexandrina	Latin America	Defender of Men
Alexiah	Latin America	Angel from heaven
Alexondra	Latin America	Defender of men
Alida	Latin America	A small-winged
Alishia	Latin America	Derived from Alicia
Alisia	Latin America	Derived from Alice
Alizabeth	Latin America	Precious
Allegra	Latin America	Joy
Allina	Latin America	Noble
Allisandra	Latin America	Of great nature
Alma	Latin America	Soul
Aloma	Latin America	Dove
Alroy	Latin America	Royal
Aluid	Latin America	Winged
Alvira	Latin America	The fair one

BABY NAMES	COUNTRY	MEANING
Alycia	Latin America	Noble
alyna	Latin America	Derived from Alice
Alysha	Latin America	Derived from Alice
Amabel	Latin America	Lovable
Amabelle	Latin America	Loveable
Amabilis	Latin America	Loving
Amadea	Latin America	Loved by God
Amadina	Latin America	Worthy of God
Amadine	Latin America	Worth of God
Amadis	Latin America	Love of God
Amalia	Latin America	Hardworking
Amalie	Latin America	Hard worker
Amanda	Latin America	Worthy of Love
Amaranta	Latin America	Flower that never fades
Amble	Latin America	Lovable
Amelia	Latin America	Industrious
Amelinds	Latin America	Hardworking
Amelita	Latin America	Hardworking
America	Latin America	Land of the Prince
Amilia	Latin America	Hardworking
Amity	Latin America	Friendship
Amoretta	Latin America	Little love
Amorette	Latin America	Little love

BABY NAMES	COUNTRY	MEANING
Amorina	Latin America	Love
Amorita	Latin America	Beloved
Amoy	Latin America	Beautiful goddess
Amphitryi	Latin America	Husband of Akmene
Amse	Latin America	Constant
Amtamdra	Latin America	An Amazon
Amy	Latin America	Beloved
Amynta	Latin America	Protector
Amyntas	Latin America	Protector
Anabel	Latin America	Full of Grace
Anabella	Latin America	Beautiful
Analicia	Latin America	Graced with God's bounty
Analisa	Latin America	Graced with God's bounty
Analisia	Latin America	Graced with God's bounty
Analissa	Latin America	Graced with God's bounty
Andes	Latin America	From the Andes
Andreana	Latin America	Strong and womanly
Angela	Latin America	Angelic
Angelica	Latin America	Angelic
Angerona	Latin America	Goddess of anguish
Angie	Latin America	Angel

BABY NAMES	COUNTRY	MEANING
Anielika	Latin America	Angel
Anita	Latin America	Gracious
Ankara	Latin America	From Amkara
Annabella	Latin America	Grace and Beauty
Annabelle	Latin America	Beautiful
Annalissa	Latin America	Grace with God's bounty
Anna-Perenna	Latin America	Daughter of Dido
Annica	Latin America	Impermanence
Annona	Latin America	Goddess of the Harvest
Annunciata	Latin America	News bearer
Anona	Latin America	Seasonal Planting
Ansa	Latin America	Constant
Antanukas	Latin America	Beyond Praise
Antoinetta	Latin America	Praiseworthy
Antonette	Latin America	Praiseworthy
Antonique	Latin America	Praiseworthy
Apollonis	Latin America	One of the Muses
Apria	Latin America	From the Apricot
April	Latin America	Opening, 4th month
Apulia	Latin America	From the River Apulia
Aquanetta	Latin America	Open the month
Aquiina	Latin America	Eagle-like

BABY NAMES	COUNTRY	MEANING
Aquiline	Latin America	Eagle-like
Aquitania	Latin America	From Aquitaine
Arabia	Latin America	From Arabia
Claudia	Latin America	Lame
Clementina	Latin America	Merciful Girl
Clodovea	Latin America	Famous Warrior
Coco	Latin America	Help
Coleta	Latin America	Victorious
Concepcion	Latin America	Reference to the Immaculate Conception
Concetta	Latin America	Reference to the Immaculate Conception
Conchetta	Latin America	Reference to the Immaculate Conception
Conshita	Latin America	Reference to the Immaculate Conception
Constancia	Latin America	Steadfast
Constanza	Latin America	Constant
Consuela	Latin America	Consolation
Delia	Latin America	Woman from Delos
Dolores	Latin America	Full of sorrows
Dulce	Latin America	Sweet daughter
Eldora	Latin America	Golden

BABY NAMES	COUNTRY	MEANING
Estella	Latin America	Star
Febe	Latin America	Brightest of women
Isa	Latin America	Promise of God
Loma	Latin America	Born on a small hill
Maricruz	Latin America	Rebellious, cross
Adiran	Latin America	Of the Adriatic
Adriel	Latin America	Congregation
Albany	Latin America	From the city of alba
Albinka	Latin America	Blond
Alva	Latin America	Fair-complexioned
Amandine	Latin America	Beloved
Amdis	Latin America	Immortal
Americus	Latin America	Royalty
Aquarius	Latin America	The water bearer

5. ASIA

BABY NAMES	COUNTRY	MEANING
Ahlam	Arab	Witty
Adila	Arab	Equal
Adra	Arab	Virgin
Camira	Australia	of the wind
Cardinia	Australia	The dawn
Htoo	Burma (Male)	Distinctive
Ba Tu	Burma (Male)	Like his father
Arun	Cambodia	The Sun
Bourey	Cambodia	County
Kiri	Cambodia	Mountain
Phirun	Cambodia	Rain
Pich	Cambodia	Diamond
Jiut	Cambodia	Rose
Aiguo	China	Patriotic
An	China	Peace
Bao	China	Treasure
Biming	China	As Clear as Jade
Bingwen	China	Bright and cultivated
Bojing	China	Win admiration
Chang	China	Thriving

BABY NAMES	COUNTRY	MEANING
Chang	China	Smooth
Changpu	China	Forever simple
Chao	China	Excellent
Chaoxiang	China	Expecting fortune
Cheng	China	Journey
Chi	China	Youthful, young at heart
Cong	China	Very Intelligent
Da	China	Accomplishing
Daquan	China	A spring
Dequan	China	Spring
Deshi	China	A man of virtue
Dewei	China	Highly virtuous
Ding	China	Born in the east
Dishi	China	Man of virtue
Fai	China	Lethal
Feng	China	Peak summit
Gang	China	Powerful
Guang	China	Light
Guang	China	Light
Guangli	China	Making bright
Guiren	China	Valuing benevolence
He	China	Yellow river
Heng	China	Lasting

BABY NAMES	COUNTRY	MEANING
Hing	China	Large
Hing	China	Courageous
Jaw-long	China	Like a dragon
Ji	China	Progression sequence
Jia	China	Good
Jian	China	Man of strength
Jiang	China	River
Jiang-long	China	Looks like a dragon
Jin	China	Gold
Jing	China	pure
Ju	China	Daisy Flower
Ju Ung	China	As powerful as a dragon
Junjie	China	Handsome and outstanding
Kang	China	Healthy
Kering	China	Cosmos
Kong	China	Sky, heaven
Kong	China	Bright
Kun	China	Earth
Kuo	China	Limitless
Laquan	China	Spring
Lei	China	Thunder
Li	China	Strong/powerful
Li	China	Upright

BABY NAMES	COUNTRY	MEANING
Oju	China	Autumn
Park	China	Cypress tree
Peng	China	A legendary bird
Renshu	China	Benevolent forbearance
Ru	China	Scholar
Yu	China	Universe
Ai	China	Lovable
Biyu	China	Jasper, the precious
Bo	China	Precious
Chan	China	Snow
Chow	China	Summer
Ehuang	China	Beautiful, August
Fang	China	Fragrant
Far	China	Flower
Genji	China	Gold
Jia	China	Beautiful
Jia-Li	China	Good and beautiful
Jiao	China	Dainty, lovely
Jiaying	China	Household flourishing
Jie	China	Pure
Jing	China	Stillness, luxuriance
Li hua	China	Beautiful flower
Lien	China	Lotus

BABY NAMES	COUNTRY	MEANING
Liling	China	White jasmine
Li-Yu	China	Rainy day
Meh-e	China	Beautiful posture
Mei	China	Gorgeous
Meifeng	China	Beautiful wind
Meixiu	China	Beautiful grace
Ming-Yue	China	Bright moon
Nuan	China	Affectionate
Qi	China	Fine jade
Qi	China	Fine jade
Rou	China	Gentle, mild
Sheu-fuh	China	Elegant phoenix
Shihong	China	The world is red
Song	China	Pine tree
Ah	China	Little one
An	China	Tranquil
Bai	China	Person of Purity
Bao	China	Gem
Bo	China	Wave-like
Chao	China	Great one
Chen	China	Break of the day
Chen	China	Dawn
Chin	China	Golden

BABY NAMES	COUNTRY	MEANING
Chun	China	Born in the Spring
Fa	China	To send, pass
Fan	China	Initial, beginning
Fang	China	Pleasing-smelling
Fen	China	Scent
Fu	China	Rich
Guang	China	Glorious
Guo	China	Fortification
Hai	China	Coming from the Sea
Han	China	Country
He	China	Lotus flower
Hua	China	Prosperous
Huan	China	Fortunate
Hui	China	Clever
Jiao	China	Fine
Jie	China	Clean
Jun	China	To be truthful
Lan	China	Orchid Flowers
Lei	China	Thunderous
Lian	China	Lovely willow
Liang	China	White woman
Lim	China	From the words
Lin	China	From the words

BABY NAMES	COUNTRY	MEANING
Ling	China	Spiritual being
Liu	China	Willow
Min	China	Intelligent
Ming	China	Admired
Mu	China	Person of Peace
Ning	China	Person of Peace
Niu	China	Girl Ox
Park	China	Cypress tree
Quiao	China	Pretty or handsome
Shan	China	Coral
Aahan	China	Dawn
Aakav	China	Shape
Aakesh	India	Lord of the Sky
Aakil	India	Intelligent
Aalok	India	Light of God
Aamin	India	Grace of God
Aanan	India	Face
Aandaleeb	India	Bluebird
Aarkashan	India	Attraction
Aarush	India	First ray of sun
Aashish	India	Blessing
Aatmadeva	India	God of the soul
Aatmik	India	Soul

BABY NAMES	COUNTRY	MEANING
Abharan	India	jewel
Abhay	India	A son of Dharma
Abheek	India	Fearless
Abhichandra	India	Beautiful moon
Abhidhar	India	Who wears serpents
Abhijat	India	A person of noble birth
Abhijay	India	victorious
Abhijit	India	A constellation dear
Abhijitha	India	Lakshmi
Abhilash	India	Wish desire
Abhimakar	India	One who has/gives warmth
Abhimanya	India	Short tempered
Abhimanyu	India	Person killed by Lakshman
Abhinav	India	Modern new novel
Abhineet	India	Actor
Abhinevesh	India	Long cherished desire
Abhiraj	India	Handsome
Abhiraja	India	Great king
Abhiram	India	Lovely pleasing
Abhirath	India	Handsome
Abhivachan	India	Good word
Abhivadak	India	One who salutes respectfully
Abhivandan	India	Salutation with respect

BABY NAMES	COUNTRY	MEANING
Abhivandya	India	One who is greeted respectfully
Abshishek	India	Ceremonious holy bath
Acharya	India	Spiritual teacher
Achir	India	New
Achyuta	India	A name of Vishnu
Adag	India	flawless
Adamya	India	Difficult
Adarsh	India	Ideal
Adharma	India	Lawless
Adheesha	India	King
Adhideva	India	The supreme god
Adi	India	A form of Vasishtha
Adit	India	First born
Adri	India	Rock
Aeshan	India	In God's grace
Afreen	India	encouragement
Aftan	India	The sun
Analah	India	Fine
Cauveriranga	India	Lord Ranganath
Chaitanya	India	Energy knowledge name
Chaithra	India	First born of the spring
Chaitya	India	A Buddhist or jain temple
Chakor	India	A bird

BABY NAMES	COUNTRY	MEANING
Chakradhar	India	Vishnu
Chakresh	India	King, emperor
Chaksu	India	Eye
Chalavanth	India	Determined person
Chalukya	India	Ancient kingdom of Karnataka
Chaman	India	Garden
Chamatkar	India	Skill wonder miracle
Chandak	India	Shining moon
Chandaka	India	Charioteer of Buddha
Chandan	India	Sandalwood
Chander	India	Moon
Chandra-Gowri	India	Name of Chandravati
Channa	India	Chickpea
Charan	India	Feet
Durjaya	India	Difficult to conquer
Eknath	India	Poet, saint
Evak	India	Equal
Gajendra	India	King of elephants
Gajra	India	Garland of flowers
Gandharva	India	Heavenly musicians
Govind	India	Popular and powerful god
Guru	India	Religious head

BABY NAMES	COUNTRY	MEANING
Haseen	India	handsome
Krishna	India	Black
Mahantesh	India	God, great soul
Pusan	India	A sage
Aahna	India	Alive
Aaleahya	India	Sunshine
Aanjay	India	Unconquerable
Aarthi	India	Way of offering prayer
Aarushi	India	First ray of the sun
Aashka	India	Blessing
Abdhija	India	Born in the goddess
Abha	India	Luster shine origin
Abharika	India	One who has a halo over her head
Abhaya	India	Fearless origin, Sanskrit
Abhayankari	India	The one who dispels fear
Abhigeetha	India	Praised
Abhigya	India	Expert
Abhijaya	India	Victorious
Abhikhya	India	Beauty fame
Abhilasha	India	Desire
Abhiman	India	Self respect
Abhimanini	India	A girl with self respect
Abhinandan	India	Handsome son

BABY NAMES	COUNTRY	MEANING
Abhinandana	India	Happiness good wishes
Abhinetri	India	Actress dancer
Abhinevesha	India	Long cherished desire
Abhiroopa	India	Attractive
Abhramani	India	Sun or moon
Abjini	India	Lotus pond
Acchoda	India	Limpid water
Achala	India	Steady mountain origin
Adarsha	India	Ideal aim
Adbhutha	India	Marvel
Adhrushta	India	Good luck
Aditi	India	Unbound, Mother of the Hindi Sun God
Aditya	India	Sun
Adrika	India	A small mountain
Adya	India	Born on the first day
Anali	India	Fire, fiery
Ananda	India	Blissful
Angarika	India	Flower
Artha	India	Wealthy
Arundhati	India	Star
Ayanna	India	Innocent
Baka	India	Crane
Bel	India	Sacred wood of apple tree

BABY NAMES	COUNTRY	MEANING
Carma	India	Fate
Cauvery	India	Same as Keveri-name
Chahna	India	Love
Chaitaly	India	Name of an ancient city
Chakrika	India	Lakshmi
Chameli	India	Flower
Champavati	India	Angaraj karna's capital
Chamunda	India	Invincible
Chanchala	India	Unsteady Lakshmi
Chanda	India	Name of the goddess Devi
Chandana	India	Sandal wood
Chandani	India	Star
Chandara	India	Of the moon
Chandi	India	Angry names of goddess
Chandra	India	Moon goddess
Changla	India	Active
Charu	India	Beautiful, attractive
Chiana	India	Shade
Corona	India	Kind
Darika	India	Maiden
Dayita	India	Beloved
Deepti	India	Full of light
Devi	India	Goddess of power

BABY NAMES	COUNTRY	MEANING
Dhyana	India	Meditation
Ekanta	India	Devoted one
Ekantika	India	Singly focused Falguni
Gagandeep	India	Sky's light
Gandhari	India	Name of a princess
Ganesa	India	Goddess of intelligence
Geet	India	Melody
Gita	India	Song
Gopi	India	Girlfriends of Lord Krishna
Gunjan	India	Buzz
Gurleen	India	Follower of the guru
Haimati	India	Snow queen
Hemakshi	India	Golden eyes
Iha	India	Wish
Indira	India	God of heaven and thunder
Janya	India	Life
Kali	India	Dark goddess
Kalini	India	Flower
Kesava	India	She of a beautiful hair
Kriti	India	A work of art
Lajila	India	Shy
Lekha	India	Writing picture
Lochan	India	Bright eyes

BABY NAMES	COUNTRY	MEANING
Manini	India	A lady
Nadiya	India	Holy place
Nilakshi	India	Blue-eyed
Padma	India	Goddess
Parvani	India	Full moon
Parvati	India	Daughter of the mountain
Raja	India	Hope
Reena	India	gem
Riddhi	India	fortunate
Sarojini	India	In the lotus
Saura	India	celestial
Aditi	India	Free and unbounded
Chaitra	India	Aries sign
Sagara	India	Ocean
Kade	Indonesia	A popular girl's name
Ai	Japan	Love, indigo, blue
Aiko	Japan	Beloved
Aki	Japan	Autumn, bright
Akio	Japan	Bright boy
Amida	Japan	Name of Buddha
Asa	Japan	Born in the morning
Botan	Japan	Peony flower of June
Chiko	Japan	Pledge

BABY NAMES	COUNTRY	MEANING
Daiki	Japan	Of great value
Daisuke	Japan	Big help
Fudo	Japan	God of fire
Goku	Japan	Sky
Goro	Japan	Fifth
Hachiro	Japan	Eight son
Hajime	Japan	First, origin, beginning
Haru	Japan	Born in the spring
Haru	Japan	Born from the spring
Haruki	Japan	Shining brightly
Haruko	Japan	First born
Haruo	Japan	Springtime man
Hideaki	Japan	Wisdom, clever person
Hideki	Japan	Splendid opportunity
Hiro	Japan	Broad, widespread
Hisoka	Japan	Secretive, reserved
Ichiro	Japan	First son
Joji	Japan	Farmer
Jun	Japan	Obedient
Naoki	Japan	Honest tree
Naoko	Japan	Straight, honest
Osamu	Japan	Ruler
Raiden	Japan	Thunder god

BABY NAMES	COUNTRY	MEANING
Ringo	Japan	Apple, Peace be with you
Ronin	Japan	Samurai without master
Saburo	Japan	Third-born son
Samuru	Japan	His name is god
Yoshi	Japan	Quiet
Aika	Japan	Love Song
Ame	Japan	Rain, heaven
Atsuko	Japan	Industrious child
Ayako	Japan	Beautiful silk girl
Azumi	Japan	Safe residence
Chitose	Japan	Thousand years
Chiyo	Japan	Eternal, thousand generations
Chizu	Japan	A thousand storks
Cho	Japan	butterfly
Chowa	Japan	Harmony
Emiko	Japan	Blessed, beautiful child
Emiyo	Japan	Beautiful generation
Erity	Japan	One who's special
Etsu	Japan	Delight
Fujita	Japan	Field
Fuyu	Japan	Born in winter
Gen	Japan	Spring
Gin	Japan	Silver

BABY NAMES	COUNTRY	MEANING
Hana	Japan	Bud or blossom
Harue	Japan	Springtime bay
Haruka	Japan	Far spring fragrance
Haruko	Japan	Born in spring
Haya	Japan	Quick, light
Hideyo	Japan	Superior generations
Ito	Japan	Thread
Iwa	Japan	Rock
Izanami	Japan	Welcomes others
Kaida	Japan	Little dragon
Kana	Japan	Dexterity and skill
Kazuko	Japan	Harmonious child
Kiaria	Japan	Fortunate
Kikuko	Japan	Chrysanthemum flower
Kozue	Japan	Branches of a tree
Kura	Japan	Treasure house
Machiko	Japan	Fortunate child
Machiko	Japan	Fortunate one
Maeko	Japan	Truthful girl
Mariko	Japan	Pure knowledge
Mayumi	Japan	Beautiful mind
Michiko	Japan	Beauty, wisdom
Misako	Japan	Ocean sand child

BABY NAMES	COUNTRY	MEANING
Misumi	Japan	Pure beauty
Miya	Japan	Sacred house
Miyako	Japan	Beautiful March child
Mizuki	Japan	Beautiful moon
Murasaki	Japan	Purple
Nami	Japan	Wave
Rai	Japan	Trust
Sachi	Japan	Girl child of bliss
Sachiko	Japan	Happy child
Sada	Japan	chaste
Sai	Japan	Talented
Sakae	Japan	Prosperity
Sakae	Japan	Prosperity
Sakiya	Japan	Cherry blossom growing
Sanako	Japan	Child of Sana
Sato	Japan	Sugar
Sayo	Japan	Born at night
Seiko	Japan	Force, truth
Shizuko	Japan	Quiet child
Sigu	Japan	Moral rectitude
Hikaru	Japan	Shine
Kamin	Japan	Joyful
Kiyoshi	Japan	Quiet child

BABY NAMES	COUNTRY	MEANING
Kuma	Japan	Bear
Orino	Japan	Workman's meadow
Bae	Korean	Inspiration
Chin	Korean	Precious
Chin-Mae	Korean	Truth
Chul	Korean	Firm
Chul-moo	Korean	Iron weapon
Chung-Ho	Korean	Righteous lake
Dae	Korean	Great
Donn	Korean	East
Duck-Hwan	Korean	Repeated virtue
Eul	Korean	Righteousness
Eun	Korean	Silver
Gi	Korean	Brave one
Hea	Korea	Grace
Hee	Korea	Brightness
Hyun-Shik	Korea	Rooted in cleverness
In-Su	Korea	Preserving the wisdom
Jin	Korea	Jewel, truth
Mun-Hee	Korea	Bright and literate
Dae	Korea	Greatness
Hea	Korea	Grace
Ja	Korea	Attractive and fiery

BABY NAMES	COUNTRY	MEANING
Yoora	Korea	Enough silk
Cho	Korea	Beautiful
Gembira	Malaysia	Happy one
Odval	Mongolia	Chrysant
Myo	Myanmar	City
On	Myanmar	Coconut
Ambrocio	Philippines	Divine, immortal one
Bayani	Philippines	Hero
Datu	Philippines	Chief
Igme	Philippines	Strong
Matalino	Philippines	Bright
Rosa	Philippines	Rose
Afa	Polynesia	hurricane
Afi	Polynesia	Fire
Afu	Polynesia	hot
Aran	Thailand	Forest
Aroon	Thailand	Dawn
Asnee	Thailand	lightning
Decha	Thailand	Powerful
Niran	Thailand	Eternal
Pravat	Thailand	History
Pricha	Thailand	Clever
Runrot	Thailand	Prosperous

BABY NAMES	COUNTRY	MEANING
Junta	Thailand	Star
Vanida	Thailand	Girl
Cadao	Vietnam	Song
Cadeo	Vietnam	folk song
Chim	Vietnam	Bird
Dong	Vietnam	Winter
Duc	Vietnam	Moral, good
Hai	Vietnam	Sea
Nien	Vietnam	Year
Am	Vietnam	Lunar, female
Cai	Vietnam	Feminine
Cam	Vietnam	Sweet citrus
Cay	Vietnam	Feminine
Chau	Vietnam	Pearl
Dep	Vietnam	Beautiful
Hang	Vietnam	Moon
Quynh	Vietnam	Night blooming flower
Binh	Vietnam	Pearl
Cais	Vietnam	Piece, average
Hao	Vietnam	Rejoicer
Le	Vietnam	Good, perfect

Chapter 3: Trendy Names

Some names are more popular than others and there are some names that people at certain times love to pick out for their babies. Here are some of those names that are trendy these days and you can pick out from among them if you want to give your baby a cool name.

BABY NAMES	MEANING, COUNTRY
Aerin	Peace, Greek
Alaia	Joyful, Basque
Alessandra	Defender of men, Greek
Alexi	Helper, Greek
Allegra	Cheerful, Italian
Anja	Gracious, Russia
Arizona	Good oak, Spanish
Athena	Goddess of Wisdom, Greek
Aymeline	Work or Effort, French
Bee	Traveler, Dutch
Bette	My God is Plentiful, French
Bianca	White, Italian
Bobbi	Hard-working, English
Brigitte	The High One or Strength, Irish
Brooklyn	Water or Stream, English
Camilla	Young ceremonial attendant, French

BABY NAMES	MEANING, COUNTRY
Cara	Love, Latin
Carine	Pure, French
Carolina	Strong, Latin
Chanel	Pipe, Female, French
Chloe	Fresh and blooming, Greek
Claudia	Lame, French
Collette	Necklace or Victorious, French
Constance	Firm of Purpose, Latin
Daisy	Day's Eye, English
Daphne	Laurel tree, Greek
Dereka	Gifted ruler, English
Diana	Heavenly or Divine, Indo-European
Elena	Light, Greek
Elettra	Amber, Italian
Elie	Height or Ascension, Hebrew
Elin	Light, Scandinavian
Elle	She, French
Elsa	Of a noble kind, German
Emilia	Rivaling, Latin
Emmanuelle	God is with us, French
Fabiola	Bean, Spanish
Freja	Lady, Female, Swedish
Frieda	Peaceful ruler, German

BABY NAMES	MEANING, COUNTRY
Genevieve	Tribe woman, English
Georgia May	Great farmer, Romanian and Latin
Georgina	Yahweh is gracious, Female, Hebrew
Gia	God is gracious, Italian
Gigi	Pledge, German
Giovanna	God is gracious, Italian
Gucci	Good or Great, Italian
Hanne	God has shown favor, Hebrew
Hanneli	God is gracious, Female, Finnish
Hedi	Warrior, German
Helena	Bright one, Greek
India	India, English
Indra	Beauty or Splendor, Sanskrit
Inez	Chaste, English
Iris	Rainbow, Greek
Isabeli	Consecrated to God, Hebrew
Jacquelyn	Yahweh may protect, Hebrew
Jemima	Dove, Hebrew
Jill	Youthful, English
Julia	Jupiter's child, Latin
June	Born of the sixth month, English
Junya	June, English

BABY NAMES	MEANING, COUNTRY
Karlie	Maiden, Greek
Karmen	Fruit garden or Song, Hebrew
Kati	Pure or Torture, Greek
Katja	Pure or Torture, Greek
Alber	Sign of rich ancestry, France
Andre	Brave, French
Bailey	Steward, French
Beckett	Beehive, English
Bruce	Thick Brush, English
Calvin	Bald, French
Caspar	Keeper of the Treasure, Persian
Cedric	Bounty pattern, English
Devon	Defender, Celtic
Drake	Snake or Dragon, English
Dries	Brave, Greek
Eddie	Successful spearman, English
Finn	Fair-haired hero, Irish
Flynn	Descendant of Flann, Irish
Francisco	Free, Spanish
Guido	Wood or Wide, Italian
Guillame	Resolute protector, French
Haider	Lion, Arabic
Johan	God is gracious, Swedish

BABY NAMES	MEANING, COUNTRY
Juergen	Farmer, Greek
Kacper	Treasurer, Persian
Kaius	Rejoicer, Finnish
Karl	Farmer, Finnish
Knox	One from the hills, English
Lachlan	Land of Lakes, Gaelic
Langley	From the long meadow or forest, English
Arden	High, Celtic
Christian	Christ-bearer, Latin
Cleo	Pride or Glory, Greek
Coco	Help, Spanish
Doutzen	Uncertain or Dove, Dutch
Dree	Strong and manly, Greek
Frankie	Free, Germanic or Italian
Harley	Hare clearing, English

Chapter 4: Big Screen Character Names

Our great movie actors and actresses are so popular on the big screen that people just love having them as their "idols". Avid fans love to almost cherish everything they can relate to them and that includes their names. If you are an avid follower of some of the big screen names, you can check here to find out if their names are suitable to be given to your baby.

NAMES TAKEN FROM AMERICAN OLD MOVIES FROM 1940-1970

BABY NAMES	MOVIE TITLE
Emil	Emil Jannings, Best Actor, 1927 - 1928 *The Last Command,1927* *The Way of All Flesh,1928*
Warner	Warner Baxter, Best Actor, 1929 *In Old Arizona*
George	George Arliss, Best Actor, 1930 *Disraeli* *The Green Goddess*
Lionel	Lionel Barrymore, Best Actor, 1931
Fredrich	Fredric March, Best Actor 1932 and 1946 *The Royal Family of Broadway*

NAMES TAKEN FROM AMERICAN OLD MOVIES FROM 1940-1970

BABY NAMES	MOVIE TITLE
Charles	Charles Laughton, Best Actor, 1933 *The Private Life of Henry VIII*
Clark	Clark Gable, Best Actor, 1934 *It Happened One Night*
Victor	Victor Mc. Laglen, Best Actor, 1935 *The Informer*
Paul	Paul Muni, Best Actor, 1936 The Life of Emile Zola
Spencer	Spencer Tracy, Best Actor, 1937 & 1938 *Boys Town*
Robert	Robert Donat, Best Actor, 1939 *Goodbye, Mr. Chips*
James	James Stuart, Best Actor, 1940 *The Philadelphia Story*
Gary	Gary Cooper, Best Actor, 1941 & 1952 *Sergeant York*
James	James Cagney, Best Actor, 1942 *Yankee Doodle Dandy*
Paul	Paul Lukas, Best Actor, 1943 *Watch on the Rhine*
Bing	Bing Crosby, Best Actor, 1944 *Going My Way*
Ray	Ray Milland, Best Actor, 1945 *The Lost Weekend*
Ronald	Ronald Colman, Best Actor, 1947 *A Double Life*

NAMES TAKEN FROM AMERICAN OLD MOVIES FROM 1940-1970

BABY NAMES	MOVIE TITLE
Laurence	Laurence Olivier, Best Actor, 1946 *Henry V*
Broderick	Broderick Crawford, Best Actor, 1949 *All the King's Men*
Jose	José Ferrer, Best Actor, 1950 *Cyrano de Bergerac*
Humphrey	Humphrey Bogart, Best Actor, 1951 *The African Queen*
William	William Holden, Best Actor, 1953 *Stalag 17*
Marlon	Marlon Brando, Best Actor, 1954 & 1972 *On the Waterfront* *The Godfather*
Ernest	Ernest Borgnine, Best Actor, 1955 *Marty*
Yul	Yul Brynner, Best Actor, 1956 *The King and I*
Alec	Alec Guinness, Best Actor, 1957 *The Bridge on the River Kwai*
David	David Niven, Best Actor, 1958 *Separate Tables*
Charlton	Charlton Heston, Best Actor, 1959 *Ben-Hur*

NAMES TAKEN FROM AMERICAN OLD MOVIES FROM 1940-1970

BABY NAMES	MOVIE TITLE
Burt	Burt Lancaster, Best Actor, 1960 *Elmer Gantry*
Maximillian	Maximilian Schell, Best Actor, 1961 *Judgment at Nuremberg*
Gregory	Gregory Peck, Best Actor, 1962 *To Kill a Mockingbird*
Sidney	Sidney Poitier, Best Actor, 1963 *Lilies of the Field*
Rex	Rex Harrison, Best Actor, 1964 *My Fair Lady*
Lee	Lee Marvin, Best Actor, 1965 *Cat Ballou*
Paul	Paul Scofield, Best Actor, 1966 *A Man for All Season*
Rod	Rod Steiger, Best Actor, 1967 *In the Heat of the Night*
Cliff	Cliff Robertson, Best Actor, 1968 *Charly*
John	John Wayne, Best Actor, 1969 *True Gift*
George	George C. , Best Actor, 1970 *Patton*

NAMES TAKEN FROM TV SHOWS

BABY NAMES	TV SHOW NAME
Laurel	Arrow
Kara	Battlestar Galactica
Rainbow	Black-ish

NAMES TAKEN FROM TV SHOWS

BABY NAMES	TV SHOW NAME
Temperance	Bones
Lainie	Castle
Bree	Desperate Housewives
Gabrielle	Desperate Housewives
Violet	Downtown Abbey
Tyra	Friday Lights Nights
Landry	Friday Night Lights
Joey	Friends
Phoebe	Friends
Jon	Game of Thrones
Marnie	Girls
Hannah	Girls
Izzie	Grey's Anatomy
Kono	Hawaii Five-O
Remy	House
Boone	Lost
Betty	Mad Men
Joan	Mad Men
Alex	Modern Family
Gloria	Modern Family
Haley	Modern Family
Ziva	NCIS

NAMES TAKEN FROM TV SHOWS

BABY NAMES	TV SHOW NAME
Peyton	One Tree Hill
Piper	Orange is the New Black
Leslie	Parks and Recreation
Ezra	Pretty Little Liars
Jenna	Pretty Little Liars
Rhoda	Rhoda
Roseanne	Roseanne
Abby	Scandal
Olivia	Scandal
Elaine	Seinfeld
Opie	The Andy Griffith Show
Bernadette	The Big Bang Theory
Penny	The Big Bang Theory
Sheldon	The Big Bang Theory
Elizabeth	The Blacklist
Arya	The Games of Thrones
Alicia	The Good Wife
Cary	The Good Wife
Grace	The Good Wife
Kalinda	The Good Wife
Carmela	The Sopranos
Maggie	The Walking Dead

NAMES TAKEN FROM TV SHOWS

BABY NAMES	TV SHOW NAME
Michinne	The Walking Dead
Fox	The X Files
Cora	Dawton Abbey
Cersei	Game of Thrones
Claire	Modern Family
Carrie	Sex in the City
Sun	(Male) Lost
Dixon	90210
Oliver	Arrow
Saul	Better Call/Breaking Bas
Andre	Black -ish
Skyler	Breaking Bad
Rupert	Buffy the Vampire Slayer
Gil	CSI
Eddie	Desperate Housewives
Frasier	Frasier
Bran	Game of Thrones
Jaime	Game of Thrones
Sansa	Game of Thrones
Tyrion	Game of Thrones
Gregory	House
Sawyer	Lost

NAMES TAKEN FROM TV SHOWS

BABY NAMES	TV SHOW NAME
Angus	MacGyver
Don	Mad Men
Bertram	Man Men
Cameron	Modern Family
Jay	Modern Family
Mitchell	Modern Family
Phil	Modern Family
Adrian	Monk
Brody	One Life to Live
Caleb	Pretty Little Liars
Spencer	Pretty Little Liars
Cyrus	Scandal
Huck	Scandal
Elliot	Scrubs
Gordon	Sesame Street
Standford	Sex and the City
Leonard	The Big Bang Theory
Raymond	The Blacklist
Marcus	The Brady Bunch
Will	The Good Wife
Axl	The Middle
Glenn	The Walking Dead

NAMES TAKEN FROM TV SHOWS

BABY NAMES	TV SHOW NAME
Rick	The Walking Dead
Shane	Weeds
Chandler	Friends
Creed	The Office

NAMES TAKEN FROM BEST MOVIES OF ALL TIMES

BABY NAMES	MOVIE TITLE
Sara	Adventures in Babysitting
Paula	An Officer and a Gentleman
Lorraine	Back to the Future
Barney	Barney and Friends
Cindy	Can't Buy Me Love
Penny	Dirty Dancing
Linda	Fast Time at Ridgemont High
Stacy	Fast Times at Ridgemont High
Cameron	Ferris Bueller's Day Off
Alex	Flashdance
Ariel	Footloose
Amsterdam	Gang of New York
Janey	Girls Just Want to Have Fun
Lynne	Girls Just Want to Have Fun
Scarlett	Gone with the Wind

NAMES TAKEN FROM BEST MOVIES OF ALL TIMES

BABY NAMES	MOVIE TITLE
Hermione	Harry Potter
Heather	Heathers
Veronica	Heathers
Abby	Let Me In
Arwen	Lord of the Rings
Sophie	Mamma Mia
Emmy	Mannequin
Jojo	Mystic Pizza
Kat	Mystic Pizza
Angelica	Pirate of the Carribean
Andie	Pretty in Pink
Blane	Pretty in Pink
Evelyn	Salt
Diane	Say Anything
Ramona	Scott Pilgrim vs. the World
Caroline	Sixteen Candles
Samantha	Sixteen Candles
Madison	Splash
Amidala	Star Wars
Leia	Star Wars
Aurora	Term of Endearment

NAMES TAKEN FROM BEST MOVIES OF ALL TIMES

BABY NAMES	MOVIE TITLE
Molly	The Brat Pack
Allison	The Breakfast Club
Allison	The Breakfast Club
Claire	The Breakfast Club
Allie	The Notebook
Tiana	The Princess and the Frog
Buttercup	The Princess Bride
Samara	The Ring
Thelma	Thelma and Louise
Rose	Titanic
Selene	Underworld
Akasha	Vampire Chronicles
Mariska	Van Helsing
June	Walk the Line
Sally	When Harry Met Sally
Tess	Working Girl
Katharine	Working Girls
Daisy	Mystic Pizza
Chris	Adventures in Baby Sitting
Daryl	Adventures in Baby Sitting
Brad Anderson	Adventures in Babysitting

NAMES TAKEN FROM BEST MOVIES OF ALL TIMES

BABY NAMES	MOVIE TITLE
Azrael	Angel of Death
Eren	Attack on Titan
Jake	Avatar
Marty	Back to the Future
Bonnie	Bonnie and Clyde
Ronald	Can't Buy Me Love
Aslan	Chronicles of Narnia
Francis	Dirty Dancing
Johnny	Dirty Dancing
Loyatt	Easy Rider
Jeff	Fast Times at Ridgemont High
Ferris	Ferris Bueller's Day Off
Sloane	Ferris Bueller's Day Off
Christian	Fifty Shades of Grey
Nick	Flashdance
Ren	Footloose
Dibbs	Game of Thrones
Stannis	Game of Thrones
Draco	Harry Potter
J.D.	Heathers
Tony	Iron Man

NAMES TAKEN FROM BEST MOVIES OF ALL TIMES

BABY NAMES	MOVIE TITLE
Frodo	Lord of the Rings
Galadriel	Lord of the Rings
Max	Mad Max
Shannon	Mamma Mia
Jonathan	Mannequin
Barbarossa	Pirates of the Caribbean
Corey	Say Anything
Lloyd	Say Anything
Mike	Sixteen Candles
Allen	Splash
Luke	Star Wars
Clark	Superman
Garret	Term of Endearment
Brian	The Breakfast
Andrew	The Breakfast Club
John	The Breakfast Club
Andy	The Goonies
Brand	The Goonies
Gatsby	The Great Gatsby
Nero	The Matrix
Noah	The Notebook

NAMES TAKEN FROM BEST MOVIES OF ALL TIMES

BABY NAMES	MOVIE TITLE
Jack Jericho	The Pick-up Artist
Jake	The Pick-up Artist
Randy	The Pick-Up Artist
Naveen	The Princess and the Frog
Elmo	The Sesame Street
Charlie	Top Gun
Maverick	Top Gun
Sam	Transformer
Lucian	Underworld
Russell	Up
Van	Van Helsing
Johnny	Walk the Line
Bjergen	Wayne's World
Harry	When Harry Met Sally
Daisy	The Great Gatsby
Daniel	The Karate Kid

Chapter 5: Mix the Gender

Names can be confusing when they seem to be interchangeable in use regardless of gender, e.g. when a boy's name is used by a girl or when it sounds like it's more suitable for a girl. The same thing works for the opposite. But what is even more surprising than hearing names that do not seem to denote a gender. These names can be used by both sexes.

A BOY'S NAME FOR A GIRL

BABY NAMES	MEANING AND ORIGINS
Barry	Irish. **Fair-haired**
Billy	English. **Resolute protector**
Bobbie	German. **Famed, bright**
Clyde	Scottish. *River*
Curtis	English. **Polite or well-bred**
Dylan	Welsh. **Son of the wave**
Jessie	Hebrew. *Wealthy*
Joey	Hebrew. **May Jehovah add or increase**
Jude	Hebrew. *Praise*
Robin	French. *Fame*

A GIRL'S NAME FOR A BOY

BABY NAMES	MEANING AND ORIGINS
Amari	African. **Strength**
Angel	Greek. **Messenger**
Artie	American. **Noble, courageous**
Ash	Hebrew. **Happy**
Aspen	American. **Aspen tree**
Aubrey	English. Fair ruler of the little people
August	German. Majestic dignity
Avery	English. Wise counselor
Bailey	English. **Bailiff**
Bay	English. Auburn-haired
Carey	Irish. **Dark or black**
Cortney	English. **Lives in the court**
Frankie	French. **Free one**
Phoenix	Greek. **Respectable, mythical bird**
Toby	English. **Good is Yahweh**

UNISEX NAMES

BABY NAMES	MEANING AND ORIGIN
Abimbola	African. **Born wealthy**
Abimbola	African. **Born wealthy**
Almas	Arabic. **Diamond**
Amal	Arabic. **Hope**

UNISEX NAMES

BABY NAMES	MEANING AND ORIGIN
Amets	Basque. *Dream*
Abiodun	*Born on a festival*
Abiodun	*Born on a festival*
An	Chinese or Vietnamese. *Peace*
Brook	English. *One living near a brook*
Addison	English. *Son of Adam*
Addison	English. *Son of Adam*
Amit	Hebrew. *Friend*
Ananta	India. *Infinite, endless*
Chanda	Indian. *Fierce*
Carey	Irish. *Descendant*
Ailbhe	Irish. *White*
Ailbhe	Irish. *White*
Akira	Japan. *Bright*
Akira	Japan. *Bright*
Chan	Khmer. *Moon*
Blair	Scottish. *Plain*
Burcin	Turkish. *Hind, doe*
Aeron	Welsh. *Berry*
Aeron	Welsh. *Berry*
Caron	Welsh. *To love*

Chapter 6: Heroine Names

All throughout history, women also got their fair share of courageous deeds. Even television shows with cartoon characters, movies, and real life personalities are great depictions that women had played active roles that were once played exclusively by their counterpart. Here are some heroine names you might want consider naming your child after.

HEROIN CARTOON CHARACTER'S NAMES

BABY NAMES	CARTOON CHARACTER
Abigail	Monster University
Alice	Alice in the Wonderland
Barbie	Toy Story 2 & 3
Blossom	Power Puff Girls
Bubbles	Power Puff Girls
Buttercup	Power Puff Girls
Colette	Ratatouille
Coral	Finding Nemo
Deb	Finding Nemo
Dolly	Toy Story 3
Dorothy	Wizard of Oz
Kagome	Inuyasha
Kim	Kim Possible

HEROIN CARTOON CHARACTER'S NAMES

BABY NAMES	CARTOON CHARACTER
Lara	Tom Raider
Mikasa	Attack on Titan
Sakura	Card Captor Sakura

INFLUENTIAL WOMAN'S NAMES

BABY NAMES	Influential women name
Angelina	Angelina Jolie
Cory	Corazon Aquino
Eleanor	Eleanor Roosevelt
Elizabeth	Queen Elizabeth
Elizabeth	Elizabeth I
Emily	Emily Dickinson
Emma	Emma Watson
Hilary	Hilary Clinton
Joan	Joan of Arc
Margaret	Margaret Thatcher
Michelle	Michelle Obama

BABY NAMES INSPIRED BY THE MYTHOLOGY

BABY NAMES	SEX/MEANING/ORIGIN
Acantha	Thorn, prickle

BABY NAMES INSPIRED BY THE MYTHOLOGY

BABY NAMES	SEX/MEANING/ORIGIN
Astraea	Goddess of justice
Athena	Goddess of wisdom
Cassandra	Princess
Clio	Muse of history
Cybele	Mother of the gods
Danae	Mother of Perseus
Delia	From the greek island Delos (Home of Apollo)
Freya	Norse goddess
Gaia	Goddess of Earth
Helen	Daughter of Zeus, Great beauty
Iris	Goddess of the rainbow
Isis	Goddess (Egyptian mythology)
Luna	Goddess of the moon
Niamh	Brightness, beauty
Olwen	Maiden
Oya	Warrior goddess (Yoruba mythology)
Penelope	Wife of Odysseus (Greek mythology)
Sansa	Tribal princess
Selene	Goddess of the moon
Sheila	Goddess of fertility (Celtic)

BABY NAMES INSPIRED BY THE MYTHOLOGY

BABY NAMES	SEX/MEANING/ORIGIN
Thalia	muse of comedy
Thea	Goddess of light
Theia	Greek titans
Venus	Goddess of beauty and love

Chapter 7: Heroes Names

Heroes, even those nonfiction ones really had their influence on some parents. Try to see if you know someone with a name that belongs to the list below. These guys surely have cartoon followers who love to reminisce their days through their child's name. No wonder cartoon characters have huge followers even among adults.

HEROES CARTOON CHARACTER'S NAMES

BABY NAMES	CARTOON CHARACTER
Mickey	Walt Disney
Ben	Ben 10
Dexter	Dexter's Laboratory
Clark	Justice League
Bruce	Justice League
Berlioz	The Aristocats
Kristoff	Frozen
Naveen	Princess and the Frog
Jerry	Tom and Jerry
Finn	Adventure Time

INFLUENTIAL MEN'S IN POLITICS

BABY NAMES	MEANING / ORIGINS
Abraham	The 16th President of the United States.

INFLUENTIAL MEN'S IN POLITICS

BABY NAMES	MEANING / ORIGINS
Benjamin	An English Name meaning divine gift. Theodore Roosevelt was the 26th president. He was nicknamed, "Teddy" and the name teddy bear was taken after him.
Franklin	Taken from the English meaning a free man. Franklin Peirce and Franklin Delano Roosevelt.
Gorge	George Washington, George Walker Bush, George Herbert Walker Bush. The name is Greek in origin meaning, "farmer".
Grover	From the English word meaning, "grove." He became President twice – the 22nd and 24th President of the United States.
James	The most common name among names of Presidents. Andrew Jackson and Andrew Johnson
John	With Hebrew origin that means God is gracious. President John Dams, John Quincy Adams, John Tyler and John Fitzgerald Kennedy.
Martin	Of English origin meaning, " a strong-willed warrior". William Henry Harrison, William Taft, William McKinley, and William Jefferson Clinton.

INFLUENTIAL MEN'S IN POLITICS

BABY NAMES	MEANING / ORIGINS
Millard	An English name meaning, guardian of the mill Millard Fillmore is the only President with that name,
Rutherford	English name, meaning, "fortress." It is a diminutive form of Rochester. Chester Arthur take over James Garfield as President when the latter was assassinated.
Thomas	With Greek Origin that means "twin." The only American President with this name – Pres. Thomas Jefferson.
Ulysses	A Latin name that means wounded in the thigh. Ulysses S. Grant. His true name is really Hiram, from the Hebrew word, meaning exalted brother.
Warren	An English name meaning bald. Calvin Coolidge was the 30th president of the United States.
Woodrow	English name meaning from the lane in the woods. Woodrow Wilson is the forerunner of the United Nations and founder of the League of Nations.
Zachary	A name of Hebrew Origin that means, "God has remembered."Zachary Taylor

BABY NAMES INSPIRED BY THE MYTHOLOGY

BABY NAMES	MYTH CHARACTER
Adonis	Handsome youth
Ajax	Mythical God Hero
Amon	God of Thebis from Egyptian Mythology
Angus	Celtic God of war
Anubis	Jackal-headed god from Egyptian mythology
Apollo	Greek God of Light, twin of Artemis
Ares	Greek God of War
Dylan	Celtic sea creature
Eros	Greek God of Love
Hector	Greek hero
Hermes	Greek God of Travel
Jason	From Greek myth Jason and the Argonauts
Leander	Youth from Greek myth
Mars	Roman god of war
Odin	The All-Father of Gods in Norse mythology
Pan	Greek God of flocks
Paris	Trojan prince in Greek myth
Pollux	Hero from Greek mythology, twin brother of Castor
Priam	King of Troy fro Greek Mythology
Thor	Norse God

BABY NAMES INSPIRED BY THE MYTHOLOGY

BABY NAMES	MYTH CHARACTER
Tristan	A knight from King Arthur
Troilus	Trojan Prince from Greek mythology
Tyr	God from Norse Mythology
Wak	Ethiopian Supreme God
Zeus	King of gods in Greek mythology

Conclusion

Having read our little book on baby names, you can now imagine how people all over the world are so creative in making names for new babies. The dictionary on baby names is so vastly filled and every year more and more is added to it when a new name or when one that you have never heard before comes out and make it to the limelight by way of television or the big screen.

Some names are lengthy, funny and difficult to say or sometimes don't seem to fit the owner at all. One thing is sure, though, your name is significant to the one who gave it to you.

While you are the one picking name for your baby, take the time to make the best choice as possible. After all, a name lasts as long as the person holding it.

Hoping that this eBook had help you picked the best one for your baby and may this be worthy of your referral to others.

Thanks for reading!